SUTHERLAND QUARTERLY

SQ

Sutherland Quarterly is an exciting new series
of captivating essays on current affairs
by some of Canada's finest writers,
published individually as books
and also available by annual subscription.

SUBSCRIBE ONLINE AT
SUTHERLANDQUARTERLY.COM

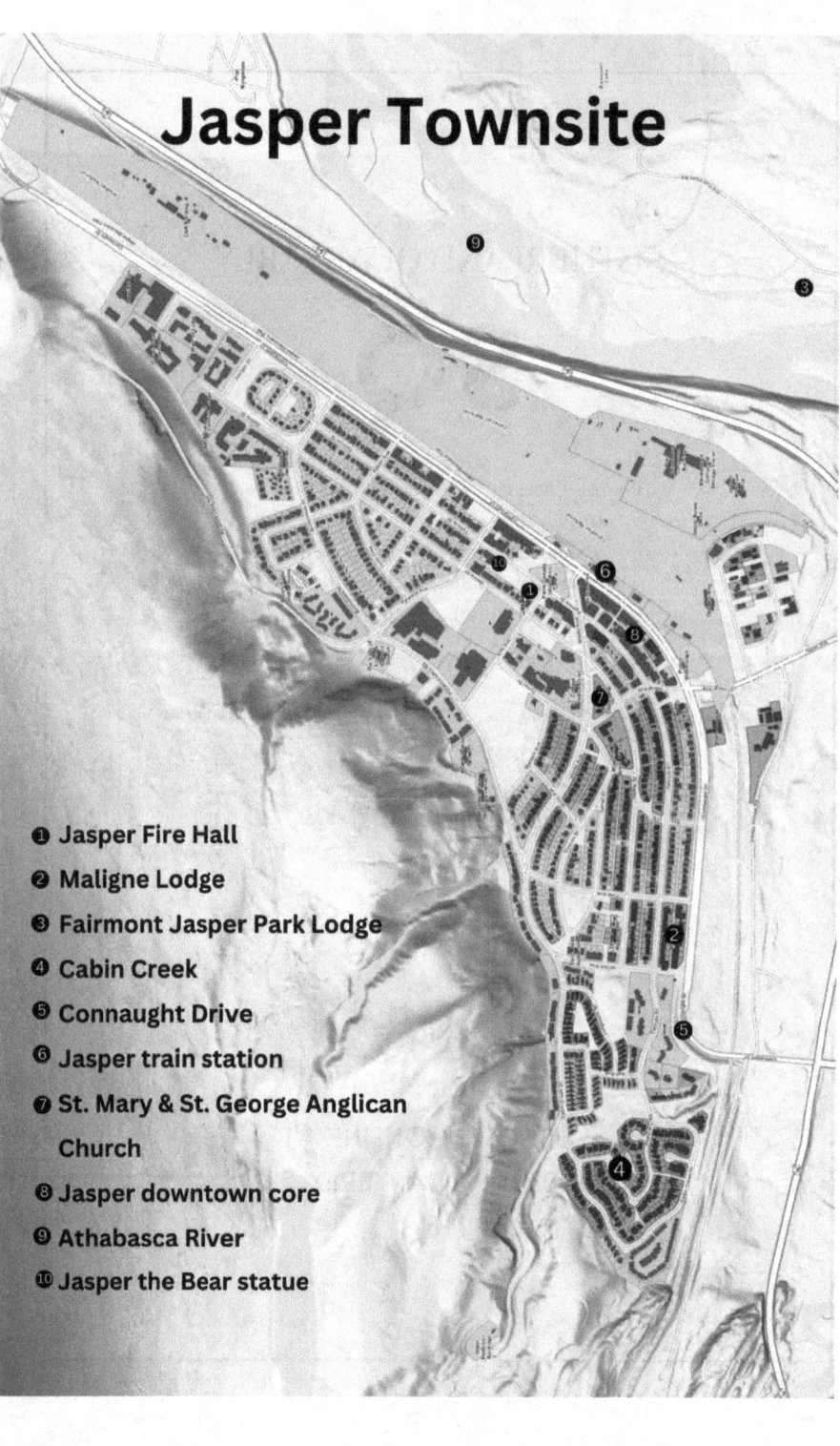

Jasper National Park

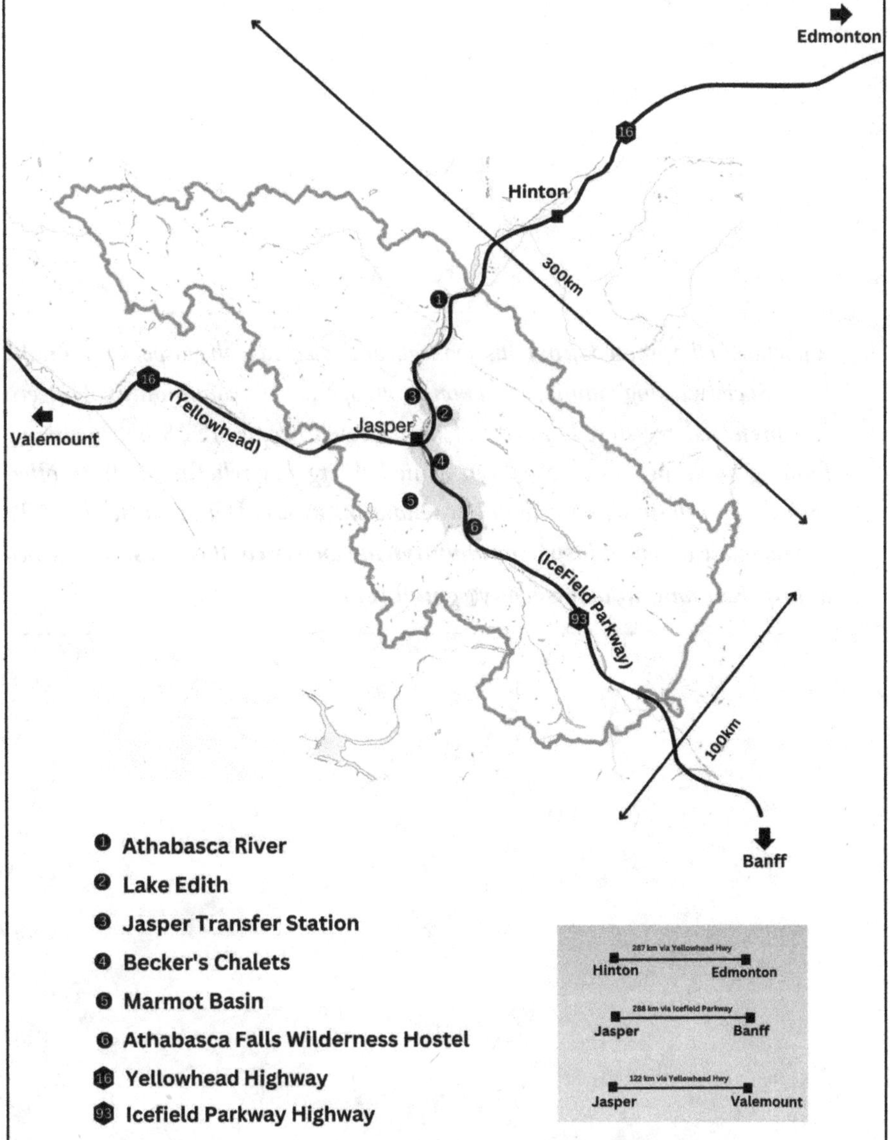

Edmonton
16
Hinton
300km
1
16
3
2
Valemount
(Yellowhead)
Jasper
4
5
6
(IceField Parkway)
93
100km
Banff
1 Athabasca River
2 Lake Edith
3 Jasper Transfer Station
4 Becker's Chalets
5 Marmot Basin
6 Athabasca Falls Wilderness Hostel
16 Yellowhead Highway
93 Icefield Parkway Highway
287 km via Yellowhead Hwy
Hinton
Edmonton
288 km via Icefield Parkway
Jasper
Banff
122 km via Yellowhead Hwy
Jasper
Valemount

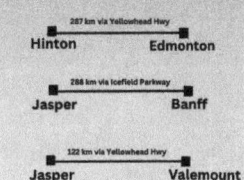

*A portion of the proceeds from this book will be dedicated to the Jasper Community Team Society, a long-running local non-profit operated by community volunteers. The preferred registered charity of Jasper townspeople, JCTS is prioritizing funding for Jasperites who've been denied emergency relief funds from other sources, and those without rental or tenant insurance. Donations to the JCTS can be made online at **jaspercommunityteamsociety.ca**. It can also be reached at **jaspercommunityteamsociety@gmail.com**.*

JASPER ON FIRE

JASPER ON FIRE

Five Days of Hell
in a Rocky Mountain Paradise

MATTHEW SCACE

SUTHERLAND HOUSE

Sutherland House
416 Moore Ave., Suite 304
Toronto, ON M4G 1C9

Copyright © 2025 by Matthew Scace

All rights reserved, including the right to reproduce this book or portions thereof in any form whatsoever. For information on rights and permissions or to request a special discount for bulk purchases, please contact Sutherland House at info@sutherlandhousebooks.com

Sutherland House and logo are registered trademarks of The Sutherland House Inc.

First edition, January 2025

We acknowledge the support of the Government of Canada.

Manufactured in Canada
Cover designed by Shalomi Ranasinghe and Jordan Lunn
Book composed by Karl Hunt

Library and Archives Canada Cataloguing in Publication
Title: Jasper on fire : five days of hell in a Rocky Mountain paradise / Matthew Scace.
Names: Scace, Matthew, author.
Description: Series statement: Sutherland quarterly ; 8
Identifiers: Canadiana (print) 2024052005X | Canadiana (ebook) 20240520076 | ISBN 9781990823985 (softcover) | ISBN 9781998365050 (EPUB)
Subjects: LCSH: Forest fires—Alberta—Jasper.
Classification: LCC SD421.34.C3 S33 2025 | DDC 634.9/61809712332—dc23

ISBN 978-1-990823-98-5
eBook 978-1-998365-05-0

***Sutherland Quarterly*, Issue 8**
Editor – Ken Whyte
Managing Editor – Shalomi Ranasinghe
Associate Editor – Leah Ciani
Marketing Director – Serina Mercier
Publicist – Sarah Miniaci
Subscription Price: $67.99 CAD (includes HST) | Single Copy Price: $17.95 USD / $19.95 CAD
For submissions and more information, e-mail us at submissions@sutherlandhousebooks.com

CONTENTS

Introduction   11

CHAPTER 1   Rare and Remote   13

CHAPTER 2   Vulnerability   20

CHAPTER 3   Hot and Dry   32

CHAPTER 4   Monday, July 22, 2024   38

CHAPTER 5   Tuesday, July 23, 2024   50

CHAPTER 6   Wednesday, July 24, 2024   58

CHAPTER 7   "Beyond Imagination"   71

About the Author   89

"It is predicted that given the proper weather conditions and an ignition source, the study area around Jasper townsite will experience a fire or series of fires that may be larger and more catastrophic than any recorded during the period of record 1665 to 1913."

—Gerald Tande, "Forest fire history around Jasper townsite," 1977

INTRODUCTION

On Wednesday afternoon, a monster loomed over the town of Jasper. It was spectacular: a towering column of smoke, higher than a skyscraper, right at the town's edge. Even more terrifying was what raged behind it: thousand-degree heat and swirling winds. It was a self-sustaining inferno, an ecosystem unto itself, even creating its own thunder.

Don Smith was too busy to see it approach. The gentle veteran of the Jasper Fire Department had been racing around town, propping up sprinklers on stainless-steel legs. The town's air-raid siren had been blaring for more than an hour. Parks Canada firefighters were long gone. Less than forty people remained in Jasper, most of them unpaid volunteers protecting homes in which they'd grown up, played as children, shared dinners and holidays, and eventually raising their own kids. Smith was one of those people.

Without warning, the smoke fell. As if tired of sustaining its great height, the tower collapsed and, much like a fallen building, sent smoke jetting out its sides. The blue sky disappeared. Day turned to night. Waves of smoke swept through Jasper's streets. Trees rattled, lurching sideways as the wind howled. Incandescent remnants of trees—pinecones, needles, and bark—hurtled overhead.

Boom went a propane tank. *Boom* went another. *Boom*.

"It was a blur," says Smith. After nearly two days of preparation, the firefighters were suddenly in a war zone. Chronological time ceased to matter. Voices yelled over the radio, calling for engines at homes that had caught fire. The number of emergencies far exceeded the capacities of respondents.

Jasper was on fire.

The town's residents had long known this day would come. It was the result of decades of forest mismanagement. It was the result of the natural processes a forest undergoes to regenerate itself. It was undoubtedly a result of conditions attributable to a warming climate. And it was helped along by decades of town planning that had made local homes uniquely accessible to fire.

All of the above contributed to the perfect storm that landed on Jasper's doorstep, a punishingly destructive force that overwhelmed one of the best and largest firefighting crews in the world. It devastated one of the jewels of the Canadian Rockies, right in the middle of Jasper National Park, a UNESCO World Heritage Site renowned for its rugged mountains, deep forests, pristine lakes, and abundant wildlife.

Jasper was far from the first Canadian community to be struck by a wildfire. It wasn't even the first in Alberta. Who could forget Slave Lake in 2011 or Fort McMurray in 2016? But it was certainly the most beloved. It is a town of less than 5,000 people in a park that attracts two million tourists a year. Even without live film footage, the fire that night was easy for Canadians to visualize: poor Jasper the Bear, the town mascot, standing on his hind legs, maintaining his cheerful countenance as his town was engulfed by flames. The site of countless memories would, many feared, be wiped off the face of the earth by morning.

CHAPTER ONE

RARE AND REMOTE

It feels improbable that a place like Jasper should exist. It is remarkably isolated. While reachable from three directions, none is an easy or a short drive.

Approaching east from BC means at least a four-hour haul on single-lane highways with a bare minimum of gas stations and intermittent cellular reception.

The drive west from Edmonton is also four hours, a pancake-flat journey across flat scrubland until the Rocky Mountains begin to form a short distance from the small industrial town of Hinton.

The approach from the south, along the infamous Icefields Parkway, is the only efficient way to Jasper if you're starting from Calgary. It is also the most treacherous route, beginning north of Banff, around Lake Louise, and winding around mountains and up and down steep inclines in single lanes for several hours. Cell service disappears early on the route and doesn't return until you reach your destination. Driving conditions, often as not, are white-knuckle—blizzards can hit in an instant at any time of year—and the road can feel awfully lonely, even scary outside of tourist season. Yet this approach is the most rewarding. Every turn is a grand reveal of some breathtaking new landscape: a wall of rock with a turquoise lake at its feet; a row of spire-like peaks 10,000 feet high and majestically robed in evergreens;

blue-hued glaciers; thunderous waterfalls. Even veteran parkway travellers still regularly pull over to enjoy the view.

Surely God did not intend for humans to forge paths through such terrain, yet thirty-foot recreational vehicles pass through this corner of the world. There you are, on a slow, steep climb up the side of another mountain, when their headlights blind you from above.

The travel required to reach Jasper is important to an understanding of the town. You have to ask yourself why people would go to such trouble, blasting through hundreds of kilometres of rock and forest to reach this tiny townsite. If reaching a beautiful mountain range was the point, why not stop at Banff, only 127 kilometres from Calgary?

It should be no surprise that Jasper, like Banff, was created by commerce, the only force that could sustain a community so deep in a mountainous wilderness. The town was unofficially born in 1910 as construction began on a railway, eventually owned by Canadian National, connecting a new seaside port in northern British Columbia to Lake Superior in northern Ontario. The Jasper townsite was chosen as a regional headquarters for construction and repairs. Railway workers rushed in, erecting shacks and encampments a short distance from the tracks.

Government wasn't far behind industry. Canada's federal government had granted itself control of the Jasper Park Forest Reserve in 1907. It identified the townsite as its headquarters within the newly established park boundaries and began formulating plans for tourism in what became Jasper National Park in 1930. In a matter of a few years, Jasper went from remote outpost to highly advertised tourist destination. Icefields Parkway, meanwhile, was a federally commissioned job-creation project during the Great Depression, connecting the Rockies' scenic trio of Banff, Lake Louise, and Jasper. It began in 1931 and was completed nine years later.

The heavy hand of federal control is a dominant theme in Jasper's narrative. The smattering of European traders and settlers that had encroached on the area since the early 1800s were relatively unbothered by the feds' initial approach, but Indigenous communities that had occupied these mountains since time immemorial were acutely affected. Viewed as impediments to the enjoyment of nature, they were evicted from the park boundaries, treated as trespassers on their own land. They were not allowed to live, hunt, or harvest within the expansive territory claimed by the government, never mind that they'd lived on these lands long before Canada existed as a country. There was not a shred of grace to their eviction. Camps and cabins were destroyed; mountains were renamed. Some Indigenous people had to walk out of the park and resettle as far as 100 kilometres from their homes.

Once it gained control of the park and its townsite and scrubbed away any hint that another culture had existed before the railway tracks were laid, Parks Canada officials sought to colour the blank slate they had created. One of the first questions on the table was how Jasper should appear to visitors and its residents. Officials were sent from Ottawa to figure out an answer.

Federal control over Jasper via Parks Canada is largely manifest today in its restrictions over the town's geographic footprint and real estate. The town has long curbed development outside its small prescribed boundaries which reach only a handful of kilometres from end to end. Urban sprawl has never been a concern for Jasper. The opposite, in fact: the town has famously sported a long-standing zero-per-cent vacancy rate.

The effects of federal control are evident in the look and feel of Jasper. They became noticeable in 1913, when strict control over the town's development transformed Jasper from an assorted collection of shacks into a town designed to suit its majestic natural surroundings. The result is a uniformity of architecture and sensibility.

Cedar shakes—little rectangular slats of cedar wood frequently used for roofing or siding—are the norm, although asphalt shingles and pre-finished metals are present, too. All other materials are "unacceptable." Parks Canada guidelines describe the overall goal: "What might be called 'Mountain Architecture' is not so much a style as a series of building characteristics." It owes more to Swiss ski resorts than anything distinctively Canadian.

Parks Canada's authority is enhanced by the fact that Jasper residents don't own their homes in conventional terms. The federally-owned land is instead leased to residents on a forty-two-year basis. It's an abnormal arrangement, to be sure. The only other town that operates similarly is Banff, where the municipality is subject to almost identical rules. It's perhaps why the two are treated by many tourists as a coin flip: Banff or Jasper?

In fact, there are significant differences. Jasper has rugged edges and smaller crowds that some visitors find more appealing than the increasingly crowded environs of Banff, with its proximity to Calgary and higher international profile. Both towns have sprawling, lavish resorts, but Jasper plays the subtly wealthy blue-collar sibling to its more ostentatious investment-banking brother.

Banff is a year-round base for tourists, while Jasper, despite good skiing nearby, takes the bulk of its visitors in the summer before going quiet in winter—hotel prices can be sliced by a third. Jasper's local Legion and its nearby residential neighbourhoods provide it with a layer of permanence and small-town affect not as obvious in Banff, which annually welcomes about four million people. The two national parks are the most visited in all of Canada.

Only since late in the last century has Jasper been afforded many of the responsibilities taken for granted by municipalities outside the bounds of national parks. Most municipalities report to provincial governments, not Ottawa. Since 1989, Jasper had been represented by an elected town committee, chaired by a man named Richard Ireland. He initially ran for the position after Jasper's first failed vote for self-governance. It failed, prompting the town's entire committee to resign. In 1995, Jasper was named an improvement district, a status often given to sparsely populated areas that lack a sufficient tax base to support a community.

Richard Ireland is exactly the type of person you'd expect to lead a town like Jasper. He was born and raised there by his two parents in a three-bedroom home along with three siblings and, often, one or two grandparents. Growing up, he'd rise early to fish in the Athabasca River before biking to school. He's a lifelong outdoorsman and has completed several Ironman triathlons; those same passions extend to hiking up Jasper's mountains in the summer and skiing them in winter. A lawyer by trade, Ireland also has a sterling memory and can recall civic events down to the date and number of votes. He travels across town to meetings and social events on one of his many bikes, weather permitting. Although soft-spoken, he has a sharp tongue when tested. Years after returning to Jasper from school, he bought his childhood home where he and his wife Bonnie have raised their two sons, Logan and Graeme. "Dick's a smart lad, articulate and thoughtful," one Jasper hotel owner told the *Edmonton Journal* after Ireland was elected.

Chairing the town committee through the 1990s, Ireland struggled to deal with issues that have become more urgent since the town developed into a marquee tourist destination. Bureaucracy frustrated the business community and residents. Getting things done was challenging; it didn't help that Jasper felt as though it was being managed by remote bureaucrats in Ottawa.

One of those issues was over the town's ability to handle local fires. A report found seventeen deficiencies in Jasper's fire department: it didn't have enough engines; the ones it had were too small or too old; training volunteer firefighters was nearly impossible given the size of the fire hall; the hydrant system was poor. The list went on.

The moment that lit a fire under the federal government, Ireland says, was a parliamentary hearing he attended in Ottawa, which came shortly after the government had bought a new Jaws of Life machine for Jasper. It was welcome news, but there was a problem: the new machinery didn't fit in the fire hall. To Ireland, that story cracked the nut he'd been chipping away at for years. "That won the day, in the sense that it got us in the doors that we needed to be in, and then we could discuss the more serious matters," Ireland says.

Jasper's ongoing campaign for a greater degree of self-governance was observed with great interest in other parts of the country. Ireland was profiled by the *Edmonton Journal*, which called him a "politician in paradise." A story in the *Globe and Mail* featured a photo of a moustachioed Ireland wearing a top hat, standing in front of a stop sign, and looking out toward the mountains. Reporters were generally sympathetic to Jasper's plight. "Ask anyone who lives in Jasper, the picturesque little Alberta town nestled in the Rockies, about the nuts and bolts of everyday life and you'll likely get an angry earful," wrote *Globe* reporter Jill Mahoney. Alberta's then-premier Ralph Klein contributed to that earful: "When the premier of Alberta has to pay $70 to get into the park to talk to his own constituents, it's a piss-off," he told the *Jasper Booster*, the local paper at the time.

Jasper had ambitions, but those ambitions had limits. While it had been fighting to gain municipality status, it had watched its counterpart, Banff, add 3,000 people in eight years. "Jasper residents don't want to end up like Banff," an *Edmonton Journal* sub-headline read in 1995, although, prior to taking control over its affairs, Banff had likewise been frustrated by its crumbling infrastructure.

Ben Gadd, an interpretive guide, was strongly against more autonomy. He felt regulation needed to be tight in Jasper and feared a local council would become overrun by a coalition of pro-development lawyers and businessmen. There was palpable concern that Jasper's interests—primarily those of nature conservation—would be diluted by development. Parks Canada was seen by some as a bulwark against that eventuality. Before the town of Jasper held a plebiscite on the question of whether it should become an incorporated municipality or remain under Parks Canada in 2001, Gadd argued in a newspaper article that if the experiment with autonomy failed, there was no going back.

The result of that plebiscite wasn't close. The town voted 1,145 to 410 in favour of establishing a local government and Ireland was soon elected the first mayor of Jasper.

The town's new status gave it a number of new, if limited, powers. A town council was formed and took responsibility for many of the jobs normally afforded to municipalities: water treatment, road clearing, waste management, bylaw enforcement, managing community centres. The Town of Jasper would begin collecting property taxes, although Parks Canada remained the ultimate landowner, continuing to lease out the land on forty-two-year terms. The tight town boundary would remain as it was. Parks Canada retained oversight of land-use planning and environmental matters through the Ministry of Canadian Heritage.

The vote changed Ireland's life. There was less time for cross-country skiing in the Tonquin Valley or flipping through novels in front of a log fire.

"I used to think my days were full. Now I know they are," he told the *Edmonton Journal* after his election.

CHAPTER 2

VULNERABILITY

"It wasn't a matter of if it was going to happen, but when," says Jasper fire chief Mathew Conte.

Ask a Jasper resident whether they'd ever expected wildfire to reach town and they'll more than likely repeat these words verbatim.

Jasper National Park, located in the northernmost section of the eastern Rocky Mountains, is a dense forest packed with a mix of vegetation. Scattered through the woods are lodgepole pine, white and black spruce, and Douglas-fir. The forest floor, in places, is covered with a layer of grass.

Jasper's ecosystems rely on fire for both maintenance and survival. Wildfires can produce a nutrient-rich seed bed that, due to the lack of foliage, is able to receive the sunlight necessary for regrowth. Some plants have the ability to regenerate their root systems even after a devastating wildfire by activating dormant buds inside their tangled webs beneath the soil.

When they're doing their job, wildfires also create little communities of trees that are all the same age, turning the forest into a vast multigenerational household. Aged forests, with their dried and decaying branches, are designed to burn while a neighbouring cluster of trees, full of youthful moisture, having emerged from destruction several years prior, is less prone to fire. When an old group of trees goes up in flames, the perimeter of younger trees often stops the blaze from getting out of control. The heat intensity drops and is reduced to a smoulder. The young trees now have a neighbour that's less flammable. And so the circle of life continues, the trees playing willing prey to the predatory flames.

The park forests have a high volume of lodgepole pine. Healthy ones stand straight as an arrow with much of their foliage bunched in the treetop; the trunks below the middle tend to be bare. Only a handful of meters separates one trunk from another, which leaves Jasper's valleys and slopes looking like endless stalks of asparagus. Without a trail for guidance, traversing through a forest of lodgepole pine can be slow and disorienting.

The Douglas-fir, recognizable by its Christmas-tree appearance, is another predominant species in the area. It is not a fir but a member of the pine family. Douglas-firs are far more scattered than lodgepole pine, although they, too, are evergreens, keeping their needle-like leaves twelve months a year.

When it comes to fire, the two types of trees could not be more different. The thick, corky bark of Douglas-fir, absent flammable resin, make them resistant to burning. When wildfire researchers set out to learn about an area's fire history, Douglas-firs are the least helpful because they resist carrying scars of the last fire. Lodgepoles, on the other hand, wear fire up and down their trunks. They're made to burn every century or so, and when they do, they burn impressively.

One study in 1977 by University of Alberta graduate student Gerald Tande set out to document wildfire history around the Jasper townsite. Tande wanted to understand how frequently fires burned in the area prior to 1907, which was around the time local fire suppression efforts began.

In that study, Tande found fires happened in multi-year clusters, culminating in major fires during specific years, including 1758, 1847, and 1889. Between those peaks, he noted in his thesis, erratic small cycles of fires occurred, oscillating in size from year to year.

Tande noted an aberration in the early 1900s. "This cyclic pattern of fluctuations in the size of past fires is abruptly lost after 1910," he wrote. It is probably not coincidental that this was the time that the outside world encroached on the region, beginning with the railway's construction, the subsequent establishment of federal control of the park, and the eviction of the local Indigenous communities.

For a study exploring a national park covering more than 11,000 square kilometres, Tande's discovery was remarkably unambiguous. The majority of lodgepole pine in the park started to grow after 1889, which had been the last recorded major wildfire up to his paper's 1977 publication. He found no trees on the landscape that were born after 1919, coinciding with the first decades in which Jasper National Park was established. During that time, he wrote, land managers in the area "tended to regard fire as an undesirable disturbance rather than a natural factor in the environment."

The potential effects of fire suppression are "long and alarming," wrote Tande. Among them are the unnatural progression of changes to a forest's aging beyond stages that would have naturally occurred. To close, he recommended what today are known as prescribed burns. These are controlled fires set "so that a more natural mosaic will remain for future generations."

Tande added a prescient note: ". . . forests of the Jasper townsite study area will eventually burn again. The longer they are without fire, the more organic matter will accumulate, and the more severe fire will be during favourable weather conditions." He further predicted Jasper "will experience a fire or series of fires that may be larger and more catastrophic than any recorded during the period of record 1665 to 1913." Parks Canada was aware of Tande's thesis. But it did not begin its first prescribed burns until nearly two decades later, in 1996.

Prescribed burns usually entail selecting an area and setting fire to that plot of land using gasoline. The fire is maintained at a moderate level of intensity so the less flammable trees survive and the ready-to-burn fuels, such as lodgepole pine, are incinerated. The primary goal of these burns and tree-thinning projects is to reduce the amount of flammable material, or fuel, on the forest floor and decrease the likelihood that future forest fires will reach the treetops in what is commonly referred to as a crown fire. Firefighters can better attack and control a blaze at ground level. There's not much they can do with a crown fire.

The project of restoring fire to the ecosystem was spearheaded by Alan Westhaver, Jasper National Park's former long-time fire vegetation expert, who served in several national parks. Westhaver says that returning fire was the "heart and soul of our program." By the 1990s, Parks Canada was well aware that the absence of fire across the national had become a growing risk to the town.

Early prescribed burns were not widely welcomed by the community, which wondered how lighting the forest on fire and sending smoke into the atmosphere fit the concept of *conservation*. Smoke does not have a sterling reputation, especially when a town's economic foundation rests on tourists who tend to be unnerved by the prospect of wildfire. Local journalists wrote stories explaining why Parks Canada was suddenly focused on this concept of "reintroducing fire," but the stories did little to improve the popularity of the smoke.

Between 2003 and 2011, Westhaver oversaw more than 1,000 hectares of fuel modifications around the townsite and its iconic luxury resort, Jasper Park Lodge. Over this time, he worked hand-in-glove with Greg van Tighem, Jasper's first-ever fire chief, who had helped Jasper gain municipality status. Around this time, the two firefighting compadres became deeply invested in a new fireproofing program called FireSmart.

There's a saying among firefighters that towns burn from the inside out.

The image most laypeople have of the wildfires that approach urban areas is of a huge wall of flame speeding through the forest, destroying everything in its path. It has the force and inevitability of an all-out blitz. In reality, an urban wildfire often resembles air warfare rather than ground warfare. It starts when the active wildfire, crackling in the trees, is approaching a community and gets within a distance of about two kilometres. Along with clouds of smoke, embers of twigs, bark, and needles are lobbed into the sky. They are carried by wind, a streak of sparks hurtling toward civilization. Those embers, showering overhead by the thousands, land anywhere and everywhere: on streets, sidewalks, lawns, decks, roofs, and propane tanks. Many of them are too light to retain enough heat to inflict damage. They are extinguished soon after touching down. But many of them retain enough heat to grab a foothold on flammable material before they die.

This is how towns burn from the inside out. It's not via walls of thousand-degree flames on a destructive warpath, but via little pieces of glowing shrapnel tossed into bushes or atop roofs—innumerable little hand grenades that can engulf a home in flames within minutes.

This sequence of events has been common knowledge among firefighters for decades. Since the 1990s, it has led some of them to advocate for ways to reduce the damage those soaring embers can have on a community. FireSmart programs are not sexy nor dramatic; they are sometimes controversial. A distant cousin to spring cleaning, FireSmart practice requires removing all flammable materials within at least 1.5 meters of a home. Of special concern are plastic Muskoka chairs, loose leaves, debris under backyard decks, and flammable shrubs, especially juniper bushes. Sometimes, the FireSmart approach requires cutting down a combustible tree whose trunk is less than a few feet from a back porch, or whose branches scratch the side of a house.

When Westhaver moved to Jasper, he approached van Tighem and laid out the potential fire risks in the town. That inventory of dangers, paired with Parks Canada's recognition of the need for prescribed burns to reduce the of prescribed burns to manage hazardous conditions in surrounding forests, galvanized the two to implement FireSmart in the town.

"To be honest, when we started, it wasn't very well received," van Tighem says. "We had a lot of people—they just didn't want to cut a tree down." Their efforts sparked conversations about the meaning of conservation. Did it require the maintenance of every tree in town? Or did it involve revving a chainsaw in service of preventing greater loss should a fire reach Jasper? However flammable, junipers are indigenous to Jasper National Park and tend to grow well in its dry, rocky landscape.

Answering that question and persuading the public was slow and arduous. Van Tighem persisted, encouraging people to keep conifers, whether pine trees or juniper bushes, as far away from their buildings as possible. He assembled small neighbourhood groups called "work bees" that would meet on a weekend morning and he'd teach them about FireSmarting tactics. Afterwards, he would send them out into their yards to putter away. He enlisted members of Jasper's volunteer fire department to help uproot juniper bushes or saw down cedar bushes, which are also indigenous to the park. A little pile of debris would form, which van Tighem chose to burn on site or take away to incinerate when conditions allowed. Those weekend mornings always closed out with a community barbecue.

"It took a few years, but we actually started winning people over," he says. One of his glittering successes was in Lake Edith, a small subdivision or cottage community outside the Jasper townsite beside its namesake body of water. It is surrounded by forest. The few people living in the ring of cottages jumped on board with FireSmart in 1998, and it later became Alberta's first FireSmart-certified community.

The first clue that Parks Canada's forest management techniques and the new FireSmart initiatives would not be enough to protect Jasper came in 2003 when a prescribed burn, which would become known as the Syncline fire, ran out of control along the park's eastern boundaries, near Hinton.

Jen Beverly watched from a helicopter as the 100-foot flames emerged from clusters of lodgepole pines and roared south into

Rocky River Valley. It razed almost 21,000 hectares (67,000 acres) of forest. Now a wildfire researcher for the University of Alberta, Beverly at the time was working for the federal government, running a new fire behaviour model. She witnessed the blaze from above, and later, once it was extinguished, from ground level. She understood that the forest had been waiting to burn for many years, and that national park's ecosystem was regenerating itself through the towering flames, but it was nonetheless alarming, even if it occurred a full sixty kilometres from the Jasper townsite. "It's incredible," she says. "It's an incredibly impressive sight when you see that."

Twenty years later, the extent of the Syncline damage is still visible from satellite images. Across from small, emerald Talbot Lake, the green forest comes to an abrupt halt. For more than ten kilometres into the valley and around jagged peaks, the map goes grey. Zooming in closer, what appear to be tiny strokes from a fine pen eventually show themselves as tangled masses of deadfall strewn across the forest floor. Knowing the forest around Jasper was loaded with trees primed to do the same, Beverly saw the Syncline fire as a harbinger of what was to come.

Sentiment regarding Jasper's risk of wildfire slowly changed in subsequent years. One University of Alberta study found locals were increasingly concerned about the town's vulnerability. People had bought into the concepts underlying Parks Canada's new fire management practices, although the Syncline wildfire, a prescribed burn gone wrong, left many people concerned about the safety of the practice.

Notwithstanding interview subjects' perception that local wildfire risk was high, the authors of the study warned, support for Parks Canada's fire management efforts did not translate into action. Only Lake Edith residents, partly motivated to protect their cottages' heritage value and united by their tight-knit community ethos, showed substantial buy-in to FireSmart tactics.

Vulnerability

And the sins of the past continued to hamper efforts to import fire-safety tactics to Jasper. Van Tighem, who moved to Jasper in 1979, can recall when the Cabin Creek neighbourhood, within the townsite near the Athabasca River, went from being an undeveloped edge of downtown to a new subdivision. Parks Canada had long been promoting its vision for what a home in Jasper should include: imposing entrances, little windows, big walls. And cedar-shake roofs.

Those light-brown shakes cascading down roofs and the sides of homes were little slats of tinder waiting for an errant ember to send them up in flames. The chosen building materials were a thorn in van Tighem's side for most of his career. He spent years encouraging residents to undertake the expensive and laborious process of replacing their cedar roofs and siding. The effort resulted in varying degrees of success. Some residents swapped out the material for asphalt or pre-finished metals. Many did not. "It was a very slow process," he says. "We did see some progress. A lot of people did change their roofs over time, but there were still a few."

Even under the authority of the municipality, which collected property taxes from homeowners, the fire department was hamstrung in its ability to force change. Parks Canada, by leasing the land to homeowners, was the lone entity that had any say over which materials were promoted or discouraged, and it had promoted the cedar shakes.

In more recent years, as the Jasper Fire Department sought to better prepare itself for wildfire, it created a map of the town's highest-risk, most burnable homes. They were identified with little red dots. There were dots all over Jasper, but mainly they were clustered in the Cabin Creek neighbourhood, where many homes still sported cedar-shake roofs. The map would prove useful in the summer of 2024.

* * *

By most accounts, urban wildfires were largely a non-issue in Canada throughout the 1990s and first decade of the new millennium. That changed in the 2010s.

Canadians—especially western Canadians—began to talk about wildfires in a new way. First, in May 2011, fire came to Slave Lake, a 7,000-person town in northern Alberta. The blaze ripped through the community with the help of 100-km/h winds. It was the first fire to seriously damage an Alberta settlement since a 2001 wildfire in the hamlet of Chisholm destroyed fifty-nine buildings. More than 370 properties were lost in the Slave Lake fire, about a third of the town. That summer, a 705,000-hectare wildfire in the Richardson Backcountry north of Fort McMurray became the largest fire in Alberta since 1950.

The game changed forever in 2016 with the Fort McMurray wildfire. Nicknamed The Beast, the fire was among the very worst in Canadian history, devastating in both its cost, $9.9 billion, and its impact of 2,400 buildings lost. Over 88,000 residents were forced to leave the city. It remains to this day the largest evacuation Alberta has seen, a horrifying example of the impact wildfire can have when it meets an urban landscape. Smoke from the fire reached Canada's Atlantic provinces and as far south as Michigan and Illinois.

More recent was the Lytton fire. A tiny village in British Columbia's northern interior, Lytton had set the record for the highest temperature ever recorded in Canada at 49.6°C on June 29, 2021. The next day, almost nothing was left of the community. The fire spread with incredible speed. The village was ordered evacuated fifteen minutes after the blaze started. Two civilians were killed. Three years have passed since the fire blew through every home in the town, and only a handful of businesses and homes have been rebuilt.

This succession of fires has become part of the lexicon, much like Chernobyl and Three Mile Island in terms of nuclear disasters. Slave Lake, Fort McMurray and Lytton are often referred to in the same sentence as examples of the ever-increasing risk posed by wildfire to communities surrounded by Canada's vast forests.

Those wildfires also changed the game for people like van Tighem and Westhaver. Van Tighem studied the Fort McMurray wildfire to grasp how Jasper could learn from it. In video footage of the response to Fort McMurray's emergency, he saw fire trucks unable to smother tiny, threatening fires due to technical issues, in particular the arduous process of shutting down a vehicle's transmission then hooking up the engine to a hydrant, all to protect one or a handful of homes. The process was difficult enough that it forced many firefighters to drive past emerging flames that would spread and consume homes.

Van Tighem's analysis resulted in his fire department acquiring a more efficient fire engine that allows firefighters to engage in a tactic called "bump and roll." This enables them to attack infant blazes without turning off the vehicle and manually running a long hose to attack the fire. The department also bought six vehicles that include water tanks and allow firefighters to attack fires while continuing to move the truck, as well as mobile structural protection trailers that have hoses and sprinklers and can be deployed to protect homes, buildings, or other infrastructure.

Westhaver, who has since retired to Salmon Arm, BC, travelled to Fort McMurray to assess the damage in person and wrote a report for the Institute for Catastrophic Loss Reduction: "After surveying the ruins of vibrant and teeming neighbourhoods of Fort McMurray in mid-May, 2016 and searching for answers as to why some homes had survived and others not, I wondered, is this a battlefield, a memorial, or a classroom?"

In his report, as well as presentations that he continues to give eight years later, Westhaver shows footage from the rear dash cam of a pickup truck evacuating the city. To the viewer's left, a fully involved crown fire is roaring through a wooded area; a motorcyclist sits idle in traffic, on occasion shielding his face from the heat. As the pickup moves past homes, the flames screaming from the trees never reach across the street to touch vehicles or houses. They don't even come close. But embers skid across the street toward the houses. Suddenly a bush begins to flicker outside a home. Within minutes, the foot of the house is aflame and engulfing the structure. All the while, the untamed flames across the street continue to burn, busily consuming the forest.

When he visited Fort McMurray later that year, Westhaver found healthy trees standing beside the incinerated remains of dozens of homes. Why would the trees, the very thing causing the wildfire, fail to burn while homes were levelled to nothing? The video provided the thesis Westhaver and van Tighem were trying to communicate to Jasper for the better part of two decades: towns burn from the inside out, not from the outside in.

After studying the Fort McMurray wildfire, Westhaver came to a harsh conclusion at the end of his report: "Home survival was not random." Only a handful of buildings were ignited due to direct contact with flames or radiant heat, he wrote, while embers were responsible for the large majority of losses. "Again, again and again, this is the pattern that we see," he says. "The homes are the red circles and the forest around them, even on a fairly steep slope, is still there."

In 2021, when van Tighem retired from the fire department, fire still hadn't struck Jasper. But wildfire conditions were getting worse across Canada. In 2017 and 2018, the country suffered its worst wildfire seasons on record, easily surpassing one million hectares burned in British Columbia alone. The last time the province burned more than 500,000 hectares in one year was 1962.

In 2023, Jasper was included in another study looking at the vulnerability of numerous communities to urban wildfires. Jen Beverly, who had surveyed the Syncline fire twenty-one years before, led the part of the study that used a relatively simple model: it looked out from a central point of town and slowly, degree by degree, turned in a 360-degree circle. With each single-degree increment, she and researchers mapped out pathways through which a wildfire could encroach on the townsite.

Compared to other urban areas, assessing Jasper was relatively uncomplicated. Wildfires traverse valleys with ease. Jasper is surrounded by valleys; they are visible even to the untrained eye. This put the townsite at a natural disadvantage, one compounded by the fact that its forests—which, again, are supposed to burn on a regular basis—had not burned in a long time. It was apparent to Beverly that Jasper was uniquely at risk. It had 136 "viable directional trajectories between five and fifteen kilometres from town." At the end of the study, Beverly and a colleague ranked Jasper third out of more than 1,500 Alberta communities for wildfire risk, sitting behind only the tiny hamlet of Nordegg, forty-five kilometres from Banff National Park, and Hinton, sixteen kilometres from Jasper National Park.

"Every time I drove down Icefields Parkway," Beverly recalled, "I'd say, 'Wow, this is all ready to burn.'"

CHAPTER 3

HOT AND DRY

Confidence that Jasper could avoid a fire catastrophe was not high leading into the spring and summer of 2024. There was fear. There was cynicism. For people who had now lived through several intense summers of Alberta wildfire, there was a sense of fatalism, a worry that the script already had been written. All of it was justified.

In May, when weather warms and forests dry and wildfires first begin to kick up in Alberta, western Canadians were barely six months removed from the most devastating wildfire season on record. In Alberta alone, wildfires had burned an estimated 22 million hectares (54 million acres), an area bigger than England. The previous record for total area burned in a season had been shattered. In fact, it was more than doubled. Across Canada, more than 200 communities were evacuated because of wildfires. Smoke hovered over entire provinces and states like a weighted blanket; it crossed borders, even oceans.

The 2023, wildfires supported the most ominous predictions that climate scientists had been warning of for years. The change that year was not the number of wildfires—about 1,100 were recorded, consistent with recent decades—but their intensity. In post-mortems, it was determined that thirty-six fires, a number far greater than normal, accounted for 95 percent of the total area burned.

Under a changing climate, seemingly random occurrences become more regular. In summer 2023, half of those large fires, classified by

Beverly as greater than 10,000 hectares, happened in early May. That month is often a busy time for Alberta wildfire fighters due to dryness, but she found the violent outbreak of wildfire was created mostly by lightning. "This is really, really, really unusual," says Beverly. Troughs of data confirmed to her that even in exceptional years such as 1993, when lightning caused a similar number of fires, none of them turned into serious blazes.

Nature has a way of checking itself: although early spring is a risky wildfire period, the cooler temperatures are less conducive to lightning. Most wildfires that occur early in the season are started by humans—perhaps an errant cigarette or fast-spinning rubber tires in yellow grass. Later in the summer, when landscapes green up and lightning starts to flash with greater frequency, those flames are less potent due to the moisture in the flora. (Warmer spring temperatures haven't yet coincided with an early green-up, Beverly notes.) But the recent increase in temperature produced a bone-dry province—a vulnerable target with no defence mechanisms. "There's no check and balance. It doesn't have any constraints," says Beverly.

With these conditions, Alberta, Canada, and much of the United States were covered by thick clouds of smoke. An apocalyptic orange haze was cast over cities. Otherwise sunny days turned grey. Everything smelled like fire weather. And so the summer proceeded, flaring and receding, but never ending. Homes in Kelowna, BC were destroyed in a red-hot fire that was visible from across Okanagan Lake. Locals sat on park benches to watch the flames light up the night sky. Thousands of residents in forest-surrounded Indigenous reserves were forced to flee their traditional lands down bumpy dirt roads.

The 2023 fire season was not unexpected: the past seven years had produced five of the most damaging fire seasons in decades. Researchers had been predicting for years that wildfire seasons were on track to get longer. Even so, as Beverly wrote in a later peer-reviewed study, Alberta's 2023 season was anomalous. This was partly due to overlapping weather patterns, but it also "redefined what is possible under a warming climate." It was the year in which the world, or Canada, as least, entered the next geologic epoch—what author Stephen Pyne recently called The Pyrocene. Humanity was encountering a new age of fire.

By September 2023, the Canadian prairies, that vast expanse including Alberta, Saskatchewan, and Manitoba, had been locked in a multi-year drought that was only worsening. Some livestock farmers were prompted to sell portions of their cattle herds because of a poor growing season for cattle feed; governments stepped in to help them with recovery funding, calling it a "once-in-fifteen-year" program. The last time they'd issued the same support? Two years before.

As summer came to a close, 73 percent of the prairies were considered to be in some form of drought, as was 85 percent of its agricultural landscape. Agriculture Canada's monthly evaluations reported "significant precipitation deficits" and "depleted soil moisture." Rivers ran low and several water shortage advisories were issued in southern Alberta where drought hit worst, including Calgary, Alberta's most populous city. Calgary residents, drawing their water from two major glacier-fed water sources, the Bow and Elbow rivers, were limited to using outdoor sprinklers once a week for a maximum of two hours. "This is an issue of quantity, not quality," the City of Calgary wrote in its warning to residents.

The thing about drought is that it can't be erased by a single rainy season. It requires the well-timed cooperation of fall, winter, and spring in neat succession. Fall tends to be the unsung hero in this equation for hydrologists. Between August and freeze-up, they will usually be able to determine flood and river levels for the following year based on the amount of rainfall in that season. The experts like to call it antecedent moisture.

"It's like priming the system right in the same way that we have to prime a pump," says Tricia Stadnyk. Canada Research chair in hydrologic modelling at the University of Calgary's Schulich School of Engineering, she has been one of Alberta's leading voices of reason during the province's multi-year drought. Autumn rain packs in the moisture that will hold over the winter, says Stadnyk. It's a critical period for agriculture.

The province of Alberta spans about 1,200 kilometres from north to south. As per usual, rain was scattered all over its surface that fall. An Arctic front in October brought up to twenty centimeters of snow in certain areas of southern Alberta, while central Alberta, where Jasper is located, was relatively warm and dry. That rain and snow occurred in isolated parts of the province was insufficient to lift Alberta's general drought condition. At the end of October, numbers worsened: 94 percent of the prairies were now considered to be in some form of drought, including 98 percent of their agricultural landscape, up from 73 and 85 percent respectively.

Still, urgent concern was isolated to southern Alberta, below Calgary, where Canada's drought map was painted red and labelled D4, which is the worst drought level identified by the federal agency. In December, the Jasper region was merely abnormally dry, or D0, although neighbouring communities at the same latitude and only a hundred-plus kilometres west of the Alberta-British Columbia border, were in extreme drought.

The emergency arguably began in winter. Meteorologists had established that El Niño, a natural weather pattern that results in warming, and one exacerbated by a warming climate, was landing across the country, leading to below-average levels of snow precipitation. The effects were again obvious to many Albertans: handfuls of ski resorts cancelled their opening days. Alberta's annual temperature plunge, down to -40°C or lower, was interrupted by unusually balmy weather. The dense snowpack needed to eventually flood forests and rivers during the spring melt did not come as many had hoped.

By spring, the provincial government was working to strike water-sharing agreements with municipalities, industry, and irrigation districts, an unprecedented but necessary action. Calgary-based oil and gas companies, representing the multi-billion-dollar industry on which the province's financial fortunes rest, were preparing for potential cuts to their water supply. It was an irony not lost on the province that the industry that produced the lion's share of its total greenhouse-gas emissions was being disrupted by droughts exacerbated by climate change.

Alberta's water supply was viewed by many as the greatest potential crisis brew in the province that spring, but the fire hazard was not forgotten. The province's declared wildfire season begins March 1 and ends on Halloween. For 2024, however, the government bumped its start date ten days earlier, citing above-average temperatures and the lack of moisture that had persisted through winter.

Experts had also noted that the cumulative effect of the hotter, drier climate over the past several years was wearing on trees. When a tree is starved of moisture, its bark can show signs of stress such as cracks or reduced thickness. It will prioritize its roots, which are responsible for water uptake, allowing leaves to wilt and twigs to shrivel. In its bid for survival, the tree will become increasingly flammable.

Spring began about as poorly as one could expect under such conditions. In mid-May, an out-of-control wildfire in northern Alberta forced several neighbourhoods in Fort McMurray to evacuate—eight years virtually to the day since the infamous 2016 wildfire ripped through the oilsands community. Alarmingly, the fire ravaged the same area as the previous blaze. Usually, the threat of wildfire is at its lowest in recently burned regions.

The dryness was not universal. The Rockies received a welcome respite of rainy and chilly spring weather at the beginning of summer. Parts of the region were still catching fresh snow as late as mid-June; typically, bald mountains remained snowcapped into July. To Albertans with noses for wildfire weather, the spring was the honeymoon no one expected. Water-sharing agreements stood by as hypotheticals. In a perverse way, the extension of winter-like conditions into summer was welcomed by many as an improvement over the hot and dry conditions that kept people indoors to avoid wildfire smoke for days on end.

The Rocky Mountains, however, are vast, covering 55,000 square kilometres in Alberta alone. The winter-like conditions weren't experienced everywhere. Jasper was still in water debt, or drought conditions, by late spring. The University of Calgary's Stadnyk likens drought to a bank account: every six months of aridity must be repaid with six months of rain. Jasper's dryness only intensified and made precipitation more prone to evaporating. Indeed, across much of Alberta, water stores were so low that one hot week of weather was sufficient to reverse the gains from late snow and rain. "I liken that to having one match left in the matchbox and you're out in the wilderness for two months," Stadnyk said. "It's good, but it's not great."

CHAPTER 4

MONDAY, JULY 22, 2024

It had been stinking hot in Jasper for most of July. On six occasions over the first three weeks of the month, the daytime high reached 35° Celsius or hotter, far above historic averages which usually hover in the high teens. On Monday, July 22, temperatures in town and across Alberta were again surpassing 30°C. The day before, Jasper had hit 38°C.

In Alberta, landlocked and dry as a bone, you really feel that kind of heat. The dryness makes your skin constrict and crack. Sweat doesn't leave you damp—it evaporates on the skin, leaving salty white remnants on cheeks and foreheads.

As Monday wound down and Canadian National's freight trains rumbled in and out of town—twenty or thirty pass through in a day—Jasper residents were looking forward to the cool of evening. Many were closing up shops and workplaces, or already preparing dinner. There were tourists up and down Connaught Drive, which runs parallel to the tracks and serves as Jasper's commercial hub. CanaDream recreational vehicles filled parking lots. Many of the visitors were campers who had pitched their tents at nearby full-capacity campsites. Notwithstanding the heat, it was a beautiful summer day in one of the most spectacular mountain communities in Canada, and no one, not the locals or the tourists, suspected anything was amiss.

In late-afternoon, Parks Canada had called firefighters near the Jasper Transfer Station, a waste management facility, a short ten-kilometre drive north of town. There had been a number of wildfires in the vicinity throughout the month. Over the weekend, two fires south of town had been extinguished.

A crew of Jasper firefighters drove out to assist with the grass fire, joining a group of Parks Canada firefighters already on the scene and using helicopters with water buckets to douse the flames. What started out as a low-key smouldering blaze was in five minutes the size of a city park. In twenty minutes, it had jumped the highway. This fire would become known as the north fire.

Jasper fire chief Mathew Conte and his deputy chief, Don Smith, were among those early to the scene of the north fire. They could see that the helicopters were accomplishing nothing. The fire had spread from the grass into forested areas. The tops of trees were lighting up like candlesticks. The winds, at least, were blowing north, away from town and toward Hinton, sending flames toward forest that had burned two years before.

Conte had moved to Jasper just three years before, after spending more than two decades leading a small fire department in Coalhurst, a small southern Alberta town with half Jasper's population. In his mid-forties, tall and stoic, Conte carries his authority as if it comes naturally to him. He wastes few words, and those he does use are precise. For a man with several job titles that all involve emergencies, his recollection of names and numbers around specific events is remarkably sharp.

Not long after arriving at the north fire, Conte started hearing that two fires were burning around thirty kilometres south of Jasper near Icefields Parkway. Conte and deputy Smith asked Parks Canada if they should dispatch to that area. It was decided that they should stay put for another hour and help monitor the north fire, which was now raging out of control.

When Conte and Smith returned to Jasper late in the afternoon, the town they arrived in was different from the one they had left earlier that day. A wind was roaring in from the south, an unaccustomed direction for gusts in those parts. Ash was raining on Jasper, carried in on the wind.

The mood in town had shifted, too. Tourists were unsure what to make of the weather conditions. The wind and clouds looked like a brewing thunderstorm, with ash falling in lieu of rain. All Jasper smelled like a bonfire—a bit strange given that a fire ban had been imposed due to dryness, but then summer wildfires can leave all of Alberta smelling that way.

The locals had more experience of fire weather. Logan Ireland, son of mayor Richard Ireland, was at the local baseball diamond around 6 p.m. when dirt started kicking up into his eyes. Something about that wind triggered an uneasy feeling in him, and he wasn't alone. The sheer force of the gusts merited notice. "There were those dust devils blowing around the diamond," said Logan. "A lot of people were looking at each other, realizing this was a bad situation."

Most were thinking storm, however, not fire, despite the ash and dry heat. A friend of Logan's who works on pipelines said that if he were out in the field with a crew on such a hot day and saw a storm like this brewing, "You basically start running."

It was not yet obvious that the townsfolk had reason to run. People were sitting in the bleachers beside the diamond, drinking soda and waiting for the next softball game to begin. Harsh weather and wildfires have been common around Jasper in the past decade. They are something to be managed, not a cause for panic.

Still, Logan and his girlfriend, Kaylea Watters, cancelled their dinner plans after the game. A manager at the local horse stables, Kaylea wanted to round up the compound's trailers, just in case the horses needed to get out of town.

* * *

Monday, July 22, 2024

Near the west end of Jasper, Terry Chauncey and Meg Markulin were waiting on a baby. Meg, thirty-eight-weeks pregnant, had recently experienced a false labour. It had taken her an hour northeast on Highway 16 to Hinton, where she was meant to deliver. Hinton is twice the size of Jasper, with better health facilities. The doctors told Meg the baby wasn't ready but that it could come any day now. Rather than sit around waiting for nature to take its course, she and Terry had gone on one of their favourite hikes over the weekend, up near Jasper's Whirlpool and Wabasso campgrounds. They took photos of the thick forest below and soaked up the grandeur and quiet of the Rocky Mountains.

Terry is a local chef. On the evening of July 22, he cooked beef burgers he'd ground out of New York striploins left over from his restaurant. The windows of their home were splayed open for airflow; they'd been sleeping in the basement for several weeks because of the heat. Gusts of wind blew in through the windows, catching their attention. Lights flickered and fire sirens began to wail in the background. The couple was nevertheless planning to head downstairs to get some sleep just after 8 p.m. when Meg's sister called, asking if they'd heard about the fires in the Jasper area. That caught their attention.

Further to the west side of Jasper, Bob Covey, a local reporter with the *Jasper Local*, was putting dinner in front of his kids, four and eight years old, when he noticed the trees outside were swaying. He wasn't the only one who noticed. A barrage of texts was flying across town. One of Bob's neighbours had been gardening when the gusts picked up. "He was watching these trees, just mesmerized by this crazy-ass wind," Covey said.

The wind not only howled, it continued to deposit ash all over town. Residents found it layered on their outdoor furniture and tables.

The Coveys were planning to swim in the creek that evening. It was hot—so, so hot—and sunset wasn't for another hour and a half. But Bob was still watching the trees shake outside. An outdoorsman, he could tell the wind was working in unusual ways. Even the strong, sturdy aspens behind his home were tilting, and in directions he hadn't seen before. Gusts in Jasper normally track north to south and east to west, in the general direction of British Columbia. This south-to-north wind was out of the ordinary. He ditched the swim for fear a tree could fall at any moment.

Jasper is a tight-knit town. It's a meagre population of Parks Canada employees, business owners, and tourism workers. Everyone knows a guy, and information travels fast. Covey first heard from his publisher that there was a fire north of town. Word was that firefighters were tackling a blaze off Highway 16 near the Transfer Station, the one Conte and Smith were helping out on.

Closer to 8 p.m., Covey and his wife began preparing to put the kids to bed.

Around that same time, Logan Ireland's girlfriend got a call from a friend, a Parks Canada wildfire fighter. He only had a few seconds to talk. He told her to round up the horses and get out of town. Kaylea loaded the trailers while Logan packed a bag of their essentials and threw them into the back of his pickup truck.

Conte and Smith meanwhile regrouped with several Parks Canada officials, including the park superintendent, wildfire crews, and the local fire director. They decided without hesitation to issue an evacuation alert. It went out at 8:28 p.m. It was still light out and temperatures were only just beginning to wane. "There is no immediate threat to the town of Jasper," the warning read. It informed residents that multiple fires were burning on the outskirts of town.

Evacuation *alerts* are different from evacuation *orders*: an alert asks people to prepare, gather documents, pack food and water, fill up with gas. Don't panic, but be ready. An order makes an evacuation mandatory. Move now.

Terry Chauncey and Meg Markulin weren't going to wait for an evacuation order. In fact, they had decided minutes before the alert arrived that with a baby on the way, they wouldn't take any chances. Terry was also thinking of restaurant colleagues eight years earlier in Fort McMurray who were stuck for hours on the highway as the wildfire barrelled toward town, a sequence of events in which only divine intervention could explain why nobody was injured or killed.

Meg packed their bags while Terry's three-minute drive to the gas station to top up their gas took half an hour—hordes of motorists were making similar runs to fill up. Meg gathered a peculiar set of items: their cat's belongings and food, ramen, canned tuna, a can opener, their steak knife. "Pregnancy brain is a real thing. I couldn't think straight with the heat," Meg says of this strange assortment of items. She and Terry each also brought their laptops, small overnight bags, and a few pillows and blankets. Terry had the presence of mind to grab his caffeinated pre-workout mix to get through the drive.

Terry and Meg were among the first to skip town, with their cat sitting in Meg's lap. They were leaving behind the home they'd only just kitted out with a nursery for the baby. Access to Hinton was already closed off, so they drove west with the goal of eventually reaching Meg's sister's place in Kelowna. They needed a large community with a hospital that would deliver a baby. Meg was no longer going to give birth in Hinton.

Despite the ash, heat, and wind, Meg and Terry, along with many others in Jasper, were confident the disruption would be temporary. Backcountry fires had been popping up all summer and trust in Parks Canada firefighters was high. In many ways, Jasperites embodied the definition of an evacuation alert: don't panic, just be ready. "I was like, we'll be back after the weekend. It won't be that bad. There's no way it's going to reach town," says Meg.

"It seemed like a camping trip," adds Terry.

Those were common sentiments among the many Jasperites who were awaiting an evacuation order before hitting the road. Many expected the whole thing to blow over in a few days. Some treated it as a brief outing, hitching gear like mountain bikes to the back of their vehicles to give themselves something to do, and only packing enough for a few days' absence. Others were full of trepidation as they packed their cars, wanting to hope for the best, but planning for the worst.

The ones who got out between the evacuation alert and the evacuation order had a relatively smooth drive. Meg and Terry would reach Kelowna before dawn the next day after eight hours of driving along a route that normally takes about six-and-a-half hours, impressive timing compared to the hundreds of cars who would leave just an hour after them. Somewhere on that same road toward BC were Logan Ireland, and Kaylea, fleeing Jasper separately at the same time. Kaylea was towing several horses to Valemount, the first significant community on the BC side of the border, 120 kilometres from Jasper, where they would able to safely trot around.

At 9:59 p.m., barely ninety minutes after the evacuation alert, phones in Jasper buzzed with an evacuation order. If you hadn't left already, the time to get in your car was now. The grass fire by the Transfer Station along Highway 16 was running wild and continued to block the northeast route to Hinton and Edmonton. The fire along Icefields Highway had closed the southeasterly route to Banff and Calgary. All 25,000 souls in the national park could only exit one way: west over the Yellowhead Pass into BC.

Compared to the majority of evacuation alerts and orders, the time between the two in Jasper was almost instantaneous. Communities will often sit with evacuation alerts for days or weeks. If weather cooperates, fires are eventually controlled and the alerts are lifted, allowing residents to continue with their lives. Even in Fort McMurray, eight years earlier, the town had time to organize and hold a press conference before an evacuation order arrived.

This fire was not that generous. Three years earlier, the fire department and Parks Canada had used wildfire modelling to create new evacuation plans. Part of the exercise involved drawing a specific boundary around the town: once a wildfire breached the boundary, an evacuation order would be automatic. In the course of the evening, Parks Canada used choppers to scan the south valley through which Icefields Parkway runs. It found not two, but three separate wildfires. Flames had clearly breached the boundary. The first of these, near the Athabasca Falls Wilderness Hostel, had taken just sixty minutes to grow to nearly 100 hectares (250 acres).

"It was instantaneous," says deputy chief Don Smith.

"We knew that we were going to an (evacuation) order right off the bat," says Chief Conte.

* * *

Although the fires were threatening Jasper, a municipality under the aegis of the province of Alberta, Parks Canada's authority superseded that of the provincial government. Not even Alberta Premier Danielle Smith was aware of the ramifications of this relationship when the evacuation was ordered. The province couldn't send in water bombers, firefighters, engines, helicopters, or anything else, unless Parks Canada asked for assistance.

As the threat level increased, Smith asked the chief of staff for her ministry of forests and parks what options she had at her disposal. "That's when I learned—and I should have known—that we can't go into federal airspace or go into federal boundaries without their invitation," she says. Alberta prepared its firefighting teams for the call anyway. That night, the provincial government was like any other Albertan, getting the latest information from Alberta's emergency alert system and the media.

"I went to sleep not knowing whether Jasper was going to burn down on Monday night," says Smith.

Jasper's mayor, Richard Ireland, was also caught off guard. He was on a rare vacation with his wife to see their son and grandchildren.

They were sitting on a farm five hours from Jasper in Crossfield, Alberta, a suburb to Calgary's sprawling suburbs.

Ireland says that around 7 p.m. he received a call from an emergency management official to let him know about the north fire. About thirty minutes later he was informed of one or several fires to the south, but information was hazy. He didn't know their size or intensity. He just knew there were fires.

The town's emergency management department had gathered a committee that included Ireland, a town councillor, and emergency staff. Parks Canada had already signed off on the evacuation alert. Soon after, the committee, on advice of Parks officials, declared the state of local emergency, a measure that gave Chief Conte, also the town's director of emergency management, immediate powers that even the town council couldn't wield. A centralized incident management team, spearheaded by Parks Canada and the Jasper Fire Department, was automatically assembled, delegating response decisions to fire experts and largely excluding local, provincial and federal politicians.

Ireland worked his phone, getting bits and pieces of information that amounted to little more than the general public was receiving at the time. He tried to figure out a way to return home. Normally, on a Monday evening, he would have had a clear shot into Jasper. He might make it to town in under five hours, allowing him to arrive an hour or two after midnight. But this Monday, fires were blocking the Icefields Parkway. He would have been greeted by a wall of flame. His best alternative route would be to drive north to Edmonton and then west to Jasper, a trip of maybe seven hours, but the north fire had closed that access into town, too. "I was stymied. I simply couldn't get home," he says. Jasper's mayor would have to manage the crisis from the prairies.

Around 10 p.m., just before the alert went out, Ireland was advised that the town was being ordered to evacuate. It was already late, he was told, and any further delay could cause more chaos. Best to get it done while people were still awake.

In less than four hours, Ireland had transitioned from vacationer to assisting the evacuation of Jasper for the first time in his twenty-three-year mayorship.

* * *

In addition to its regular population, an estimated 10,000 tourists were in Jasper's townsite at the time of the evacuation order, with another 5,000 elsewhere in the national park. Campers along Icefields Parkway, the cohort closest to the fires, were ushered out first. Officials sent them straight out of the park, blocking routes that led to the gas station. They wouldn't have been able to access service in any event: Jasper was clogged. Almost the second the evacuation order fell, the town was gridlocked as cars funnelled onto the only single-lane highway at their disposal. Red taillights sat frozen in place along Highway 16 heading toward British Columbia.

Reporter Bob Covey shook his kids awake once the evacuation was confirmed. He packed his van with camping gear and pulled away from home with his wife next to him and the kids already falling back to sleep in the rear. The sun had finally dipped behind the mountains. Ash fluttered by street lamps and sirens wailed. Covey almost immediately encountered an endless, motionless convoy of cars, vans, pickup trucks, and recreational vehicles. The family sat in traffic just a block from home for the next three and a half hours.

Twenty minutes after the first evacuation alert, another missive from emergency officials landed: the fire was expected to reach Jasper in five hours.

"That just made people shit their pants," says Covey. That flames could reach the townsite no longer seemed hypothetical. People jumped out of their cars to run home for items they'd forgot or didn't want to leave to burn. Others, worried about their fuel levels, took the bikes off their idle vehicles and pedalled to the gas station to fill jerry cans with extra gasoline.

In the long line of vehicles waiting to leave, Covey could see all kinds of behaviour. A pair of travellers got into a heated argument, while some of the more lighthearted evacuees decided to stretch their legs, open beers, and gab on the highway. They were united only by the notion that fire would reach the townsite, possibly even where they were sitting, a stone's throw from home, before sun up.

Less than an hour later, with cars still not moving on Highway 16 west, a dramatic update: the new message clarified that the fire "is NOT expected to reach the community in 5 hours." Instead, it said, the town should be evacuated in five hours.

Covey fielded texts from friends and family. One contact told him to turn around and drive for Hinton as word was spreading that Highway 16 in that direction was now open, a rumour that ended up being true. He declined and stayed the course; changing plans would have spread panic through his vehicle, and he already had enough to worry about. One of his tires had run nearly bald on a recent road trip. Every roll forward felt like there was a softball in the tire. He'd called that day to get it fixed, but now had to flee before it could happen.

Eventually the mass of vehicles started creeping toward BC, although many in the line wouldn't get out of Jasper until well past midnight. Anxiety was palpable on the road. Some vehicles used the oncoming lane to blow by the slow-moving traffic. Covey and his family rolled into Valemount early that morning to stay with friends.

Jasper was largely evacuated within the five-hour target. By 3 a.m., the town had emptied out. The worst might've still been to come, but it felt like a major accomplishment: Jasper had been evacuated without any injuries and, all considered, in a relatively swift manner. Many emergency crews across North America to that date hadn't been able to say the same thing.

Meanwhile, Chief Conte, along with deputy Smith, their team of volunteer firefighters, and a group of first responders from Hinton and Parkland County, had been setting up sprinklers around Jasper's perimeter. With sunrise only a few hours away, the firefighters retreated to their homes for the night, some of them no doubt wondering if it would be the last time they ever slept in those beds.

Richard Ireland hardly slept that night. He had received the text that the fire would reach town within five hours. Then he had received the retraction. Deep into the night, his phone pinged with updates from officials, family members, and friends on the course of the evacuation. He waited up for confirmation that the evacuees had made it to Valemount or further. He also spoke on the phone with Valemount's mayor, letting him know that many thousands of people would be joining the town's 1,000 residents.

Ireland couldn't help but think about what awaited Jasper. He had been steeped in the decades-long efforts to ensure the worst-case scenario could be avoided. The words of a top Parks Canada wildfire official were stuck in his mind: *"The course of fire can be significantly impacted . . . sometimes."* Ireland recalls the official pausing at the end of the sentence for effect.

The mayor was thinking: "And so sometimes—is this going to be one of those times or not?"

CHAPTER 5

TUESDAY, JULY 23, 2024

Tuesday was the sort of day that ends up on postcards sold in Jasper gift shops. Winds coming from the west had blown off the smoke and ash of the night before. An expansive blue sky opened over the mountain peaks. Nothing about the weather hinted at a town preparing for a fiery assault.

The Jasper Fire Department is comprised of twenty-five volunteer firefighters and three paid positions. The volunteers are a mix of locals from a variety of backgrounds, about a third of them women. While technically accurate, the label "volunteer" is something of a misnomer. Don Smith, the department's deputy chief, prefers to call them "unpaid professionals." Their responsibilities are substantial. The fire department's response area includes all of Jasper National Park and runs sixty kilometres into British Columbia, including a number of roads that are hotspots for collisions.

Most of the firefighters huddled in the centre of town at the fire hall on Tuesday morning before continuing the work of the previous night, laying sprinkler lines around the edge of Jasper's town boundaries where forests meet buildings.

Pulling together resources and building out a sturdy line of defence has been a years-long process in Jasper, even after it gained control over local firefighting two decades earlier. But the local force is now reasonably well equipped. The Alberta government will occasionally request extra resources from nearby municipalities when it's battling an out-of-control wildfire. A town such as Jasper can collect several thousands of dollars a day by renting out either additional firefighters or equipment to the province. Lending out its structural protection trailers with their sprinklers and hoses, for example, nets Jasper $3,200 a day for the equipment alone. In 2023, one of those trailers spent an entire month in Yellowhead County, contributing well over $100,000 to the department's purse.

That money went a long way on Tuesday. In the wake of their windfall, Smith and Conte had approached town council with a proposal for the department to reinvest $150,000 of its earnings in more sprinklers. Some of these devices are no different from the simple sprinklers that flutter back and forth over suburban lawns all summer. Larger ones feature heavy-duty cylinders that feed sprinkler heads the size of a banana; they are propped up on stainless-steel legs and operate with considerably more force. Crews spent Tuesday setting up these sprinklers and industrial hoses around and atop Jasper's most critical pieces of infrastructure: the fire hall, hospital, police station, wastewater plant.

All the while, Conte was ordering more resources from across Western Canada. Fire crews from Grande Prairie, Parkland County, and Grande Cache poured into town along with wildfire fighters and structural protection units carrying dozens more sprinklers.

All the fire crews folded into a unified command structure that had been determined the night before: any department that came to help would operate under one strategic action plan spearheaded by Jasper and Parks Canada. This would seem to be a common-sense approach to coordinating an emergency response, however, it was one of the first times such a strategy had been deployed in the face of a potentially devastating urban wildfire. A post-mortem report on the Fort McMurray wildfire discovered that wildland and municipal firefighters were unable to directly communicate via radio with each other during critical junctures of the wildfire. For instance, one morning provincial wildfire crews failed to relay their knowledge that the fire would likely enter Fort McMurray that afternoon. Thanks to the mistakes of the past, Canada's wildfire responses have improved since 2016.

While the firefighters in Jasper may have been better coordinated, the provincial government still felt like it was outside looking in, even with the fire occurring within its borders. Similar situations in the past had bothered Premier Smith's government so much that earlier in 2024 it had passed legislation granting the province the ability to assume municipalities' powers during emergencies. Now, during the first crisis in which its legislation could be put to use, it was rendered moot by Parks Canada's authority over everything to do with Jasper. At Parks Canada's request, Alberta had made firefighters, helicopters, and air tankers from its wildlife service available to Jasper's defence, even though it had fifteen new wildfires to battle around the province on Tuesday. But the Alberta government was still excluded from unified command. It had no line of sight into the emergency. In Smith's words, Alberta was "in the dark."

It was a difficult position, but Smith and her colleagues weren't panicked. In fact, they were wondering on Tuesday morning if the evacuation hadn't been premature. "We were asking the questions. Did they jump the gun? Was it just an abundance of caution? Because sometimes that happens—everybody gets freaked out from what they've seen before," says Smith.

Indeed, the hundreds of wildland firefighters Parks Canada had ordered were mostly useless on that bright, sunny Tuesday in Jasper. The north and south fires were still blazing out of control. Attacking them either from the ground or from above would have been a waste of time and money. Parks Canada had tried aerial suppression tactics with helicopters and water bombers. The fires were too hot.

Many of the firefighters simply milled around Jasper, or went door to door attempting last-minute FireSmarting, removing anything that could become an ember's best friend—propane tanks, lawn furniture, firewood balancing against the side of a home. Throughout the day, choppers could be heard flying from the mountains into town carrying backcountry campers who had been evacuated from remote areas.

Greg van Tighem spent Tuesday across the Athabasca River from the Jasper townsite preparing Fairmont's Jasper Park Lodge for the approaching fires. The former Jasper fire chief had loosely adhered to the terms of retirement in the few years since leaving his post. He'd retained contracts with the town and Jasper Park Lodge as the lead FireSmart coordinator, and he spent weekends two hours north in Grande Cache, working for Alberta Forestry and Parks Canada.

Van Tighem had driven back to Jasper on Monday night when the evacuation order was released. He immediately assumed responsibility for setting up protection efforts around the iconic mountain resort, a sprawling, 700-acre campus of small cabins and employee housing surrounding an enormous main lodge renowned for its rustic elegance.

The main lodge has high timbered ceilings, grand stone fireplaces, and enormous windows with spectacular views of Whistlers Mountain, a popular tourist attraction—the Jasper SkyTram takes visitors close to its 8,100-foot summit. It had already been covered in sprinklers three months before. Van Tighem helped install them on the peaks of roofs: each sat on a metal frame, with hard piping connected to a nearby water source. Other low-profile but critical structures at the resort, such as the powerhouse and sewage building, were also pre-emptively sprinklered.

* * *

Like the lodge, Jasper's townsite was eerily quiet throughout Tuesday, its population having decamped. The same couldn't be said for the Valemount, 120 kilometres away off Highway 16 and bursting at the seams. The 1,000-person community had welcomed a population estimated to be sixteen times its size. Parks Canada acknowledged in an update that the town couldn't take more evacuees, nor could many other BC cities or towns—they were all dealing with their own wildfires. People flowing into Valemount were asked to pass through and find a route back to Alberta where they might find better support. Reception centres providing temporary accommodation and mental-health services for evacuees opened in Calgary, Edmonton, and Grande Prairie.

The Jasperites in Valemount gathered at campsites and pubs around town, digesting the few updates provided by Parks Canada and Alberta Wildfire. The mood was tense. Exhausted and recovering from the adrenaline rush of the evacuation—the momentary fear of being caught in the middle of a raging wildfire, the sounds of the sirens blaring in the distance—many evacuees clung to hope the town would be spared. They were frustrated by the lack of information available on that was happening back home and the course of the wildfires. What few details were available were filtered through spare Parks Canada communication releases. The urgency of the situation was not at all obvious in these missives. The first update came at noon on Tuesday; it offered few details on the state of the wildfires, instead outlining what was being done to assess the situation.

Alberta Wildfire, meanwhile, reported that 175 fires were blazing across the province, fifty-five of them out of control. It added that a cold front was on its way into Alberta. That was good news to the extent that lower temperatures would tend to reduce fire activity. But the cold front would first bring strong and gusty winds likely to make firefighters' jobs more challenging. "This will change the intensity of several of the wildfires in Alberta as well as the direction that they may be moving," Christie Tucker, the department's information unit manager, said in a virtual press conference. Her tone was dry, absent any sense of foreboding, but the "change" in intensity meant an increase, not a decrease.

The second and final Tuesday update from Parks Canada offered a little more information about the sprinkler lines being set up around the townsite, and the external fire departments that were arriving to help defend Jasper. The south fire was said to be twelve kilometres from town and burning on both sides of the Athabasca River. That meant the blaze was only a few kilometres from Wabasso campground, a popular site for campers. "This is a dynamic and evolving situation," Parks Canada wrote.

The park service also announced it was proactively cancelling and refunding all campground reservations that had been booked for the next two weeks. Campgrounds would need to be cleaned and staff would need to be recalled, it said. The inference was that many campers had been forced to abandon their sites in a hurry, leaving detritus behind, not that the campgrounds would have to clean up in the aftermath of a disaster.

For many evacuees hungry for information, journalist Bob Covey, who was filing stories that day, was the closest thing to an inside track. He spent much of Tuesday monitoring Parks Canada updates, pecking away at his keyboard from a woodshed at his temporary accommodations in Valemount, and posting online. Having worked in Jasper for some time, he had a solid awareness of tree-thinning and FireSmarting and related tactics that wildfire fighters deploy when a blaze is approaching. He reported on how a threatening wildfire had been handled two years prior. He told evacuees that bulldozers and water bombers would be engaging in a flurry of activity, as they were.

Beyond that, Covey was scraping together details from available sources while trying not to make false correlations. There simply wasn't much information to be had. No officials had publicly discussed with any precision how fast the wind might pick up as the cold front approached. No one was aware of how hot the fire was burning. And only the smallest group of experts understood that the fire might create its own weather system of lightning and tornados. While a certain amount of caution on the part of officials was understandable—premature speculation could damage their credibility—the general feeling among the evacuees was that they, like their premier, were in the dark. All that could be said with any degree of assurance was that the heat wave feeding the fire was expected to break sometime during the week, although that moment did not appear to be imminent.

The best thing that happened to Covey on Tuesday—chalk it up to luck or destiny—was that his accommodations turned out to be across the street from a tire yard. Between media briefings, he swapped out his bald tire for a new one. "Celebrate the win," he says.

Terry Chauncey and Meg Markulin, having made it all the way to Kelowna, had a relatively relaxing Tuesday. Hardly stopping during their drive for fear that Meg would go into labour, they had listened to country music almost the whole trip, not their usual choice, but, as Terry says, "it's kind of calming." Arriving in the middle of the night, they crashed at Meg's sister's home in the Okanagan Valley and spent the entire morning checking for updates on social media and official websites. Like the rest of the evacuees, they didn't find much. They texted family and friends to make sure they were safe. Terry communicated with his kitchen staff. Old friends they hadn't spoken to in decades reached out.

They planned to spend the coming days checking the news, going to the beach, cooking meals, reading books, and waiting for the baby. The question of whether they would have a home awaiting them when they ultimately returned to the mountains was too much to consider.

Back in Jasper, Chief Conte spent part of Tuesday evening on the Jasper firehall's second-floor deck. He had a clear view of 8,838-foot Mount Tekarra. Its base is a popular ten-kilometre hike from town. The predictive models he'd seen indicated the wildfire would reach town sometime Friday, but he could already see flames on the mountainside, candling off the treetops. With Smith beside him, he watched the fire climb from lower elevations all the way to the rocks in the alpine zone,

Tuesday, July 23, 2024

above the treeline. As it rolled up the mountain, it was apparent the fire was moving toward Jasper in a slow creep.

First responders went to bed Tuesday night with an evacuation plan in case the flames on Mount Tekarra spilled into town overnight. Radio systems and air-raid sirens were ready to be activated.

The course of fire can be significantly impacted . . . sometimes.

CHAPTER 6

WEDNESDAY, JULY 24, 2024

The several dozen people still milling around Jasper on Wednesday morning knew that a wildfire was approaching the town. The question was when would it arrive? The answer was painfully unclear. The models that had spit out projections expecting the flames to roll by on Friday were discarded early that morning. The south wind that had scattered ash over town thirty-six hours earlier had returned.

The fires south of town had merged from three separate blazes into a single monster, and it was moving toward the jagged peaks of Mount Edith Cavell, another of Jasper's trademark attractions, also popular among hikers, and Marmot Basin, the local ski resort only twelve kilometres from town, as the crow flies. It was creating a thick, lumpy, white and grey tower of smoke that soared far above the mountain peaks. It looked no different from a bulging rain cloud, apart from its unusual tint, and the bright and expansive blue skies around it. The wind was pushing the fire toward Jasper, but the smoke was rolling up into the tower, not into town as it had the night before. The north fire was meanwhile raging out of control, but rolling away from the townsite, aided by the same winds that were carrying the southerly blaze toward Jasper.

Firefighters continued laying down hoses and punching sprinklers into the ground throughout that morning. Their pace quickened with the conditions. They threw down as many sprinkler lines as possible and flipped switches to make sure the hoses were functioning. Many returned home at points in the day to pack their belongings, then settled in their cars behind the firehall to wait. A perimeter of sprinklers was mounted around them, creating a safe zone should the fire hit town.

There was little they could do but wait. The fire would arrive in its own way, in its own time. There were many eventualities and considerations to take into account. And there was only one certainty: "We would never abandon or leave," says the fire chief, Mathew Conte.

The fire kept high-ranking senior officials guessing in those final hours. At 1:30 p.m., Parks Canada communicated in a public release that the south fire had passed Marmot Basin and was around nine kilometres away. It had expanded to more than 26,000 acres and windy conditions were expected. Rain, a more effective firefighting agent than any water bomber, was also expected to arrive that night.

As the fire sat near Marmot Basin, the officials modelling its progress believed it would creep rather gradually toward town. The moment of impingement was still a moving target, potentially even a day away.

But in mid-afternoon, the fire unilaterally moved up its timetable. Aided by winds exceeding 100 kilometres per hour, the inferno began advancing on Jasper at a steady 10 km/h clip, burning whole stands of trees to a crisp in seconds. Flames flared well above the treetops, by some estimates 100 feet high.

Somehow the inferno bypassed the Marmot Basin ski hill, the most important winter tourist destination in Jasper National Park. Becker's Chalets weren't so lucky.

Becker's Chalets is a family-owned collection of log cabins between the Icefields Parkway and the Athabasca River, five kilometres south of town. Built in 1940 and originally known as Becker's Bungalows, the rustic resort became world famous in 1953 when Marilyn Monroe checked in for the filming of *The River of No Return*. Her fiancé, baseball star Joe DiMaggio, joined her, and hordes of photographers followed in their wake. On Wednesday afternoon, Becker's Chalets was consumed by fire.

Only thirty minutes later, the inferno had reached Jasper's doorstep, eating every campground, cabin, and trail in its path. Somewhere between 3:30 and 4 p.m., an air-raid siren blared across Jasper and ordered all wildfire fighters to huddle at the firehall.

Around that time, Richard Ireland was on a Zoom call with Christine Nadon, the municipality of Jasper's incident commander and head of the unified command, and Landon Shepherd, a Parks Canada fire specialist and the deputy incident commander, who was joining from within Jasper's fire hall.

As the meeting progressed Shepherd suddenly left the call, going off-screen. Ireland could tell he had received some news. A few minutes later he returned. His focus was on Nadon.

"Christine, we have to go," he said.

Nadon looked at him quizzically. "Right now?" she asked.

Shepherd reiterated that they needed to leave and had to get every firefighter out of Jasper as soon as possible. Wildland firefighters without equipment needed to go; police brought in to enforce the evacuation order and secure the town against looting also had to leave. Everyone out, now.

Conte and his team, who were staying, had meanwhile summoned nearly every fire engine within a 400-kilometre radius to Jasper. As a town with few close neighbours, it unfortunately would take several hours for them to arrive.

By the time the Parks Canada firefighters had hustled out of town, all that were left was Jasper's small team of volunteer firefighters, and a small crew of wildfire fighters. They stood largely alone, preparing to protect the town against the 100-foot flames at their front door.

"When Parks (Canada) and the (incident management team) and their wildfire crews went, 'Okay, it's time to evacuate,' we said, 'Well, we're not going,'" recalls Conte.

"That's not what we do," adds deputy chief Smith.

In extremis, firefighters could safely retreat to the firehall, which was sitting in an area replete with firebreaks. They'd wait out the fire as they would a bad thunderstorm and rush back out once the worst had passed.

The remaining firefighters were split into small groups of three or four. They careened around town in mobile units, dousing spot fires on structures. When Conte ordered them to turn on the sprinklers, they hustled to activate their systems, switching on hoses and testing to make sure their prep work was functional.

All the while, Conte and Smith kept their eyes on the dense tower of smoke at the edge of town as it stretched into the stratosphere. They knew what it portended. They were waiting for a moment they had trained for, but had never experienced in all their decades of service.

When a fire is on a warpath, aiming headlong for structures, wildland firefighters will sometimes stop trying to use water to kill the flames and opt instead to fight fire with fire. Parks Canada had imported a fire-ignition specialist from the Yukon, considered one of the best in Canada. The specialist and Parks crews tried interrupting the wildfire's ferocity; if their efforts made any difference, it was imperceptible in the moment.

Attempts to drop fire retardant were no more effective: ignition crews in the aircraft said the winds were so strong their heads were bouncing off the fuselage. "There was no evidence of environmental winds... these (were) fire-generated winds," says Landon Shepherd, Park Canada's vegetation specialist in Jasper and one of the leading incident commanders.

Early that evening, the smoke tower collapsed. The blue sky disappeared. For all intents and purposes, night had fallen five hours early in Jasper. A tsunami of blazing-hot ash and smoke engulfed the town. Howling winds bent trees sideways.

"It was straight into the ... I don't know what you call it at that point," says deputy chief Smith, words failing, giving a slight chuckle at their absence.

Brian Cornforth, fire chief for Parkland County, a rural municipal district outside Edmonton, saw the first embers rain down on Jasper. He thought it resembled an upside-down-fireworks show: the sky was shooting fireworks into the ground. The firefighters were showered with burning debris. Cornforth noticed small embers, including sizzling conifer needles, flying by, and larger pieces of the size of iPhones landing on lawns, roofs, and decks.

"Those embers were blasting us in our clothing," he says. "At that point, you know that you're going to have substantial loss."

Wildfire warfare was underway. The blanket of smoke was limiting firefighters' vision to no more than ten feet in front of them. "You couldn't drive down the streets, it would peel the paint right off your vehicle," says Smith.

There were 1,113 structures in Jasper. Despite efforts to guard many of them with sprinklers over Tuesday and Wednesday morning, crews were not able to clear every deck and porch. "A propane tank would explode, and then we'd have all that debris in the air," says Cornforth. Each explosion sent more burning shrapnel into the air.

The sheer volume of embers made it impossible to protect homes from the wildfire's onslaught. The glowing shards latched on to any remotely flammable material they could find, including clogged eavestroughs, mulch, and plastic doormats. Once fire caught hold of a house, it would break windows like a thief and crawl inside within seconds. The wind sent flames screaming like blowtorches into every opening.

At some point early in the fire, Maligne Lodge, one of the first buildings to greet visitors entering the town from BC, went up in flames. It became one of the first photos posted to social media, its cedar-shake roof and siding shimmering orange and yellow as the fire devoured it. A firefighter stood outside next to an engine, observing. The fire was inside, outside, everywhere.

* * *

The smoke across Alberta that day was some of the heaviest experienced to that point in summer, as if to communicate the crisis unfolding in Jasper. Clouds emitted by the 175 wildfires from around the province and several more from British Columbia wafted into Calgary, Edmonton, and the hundreds of rural communities scattered across the province.

At 5:30 p.m., four hours after its first update of the day, a new message to the public was released by Parks Canada incident commander Katie Ellsworth and Jasper's incident commander, Christine Nadon.

> Due to significant fire activity and forecasted strong winds, first responders will start to be relocated to Hinton. Firefighting personnel, aircraft and a small number of Incident Command staff will remain in the town of Jasper and continue efforts to protect the town.
>
> This decision has not been made lightly. First responders dedicate their lives to the protection of people and communities. Given the intensity of fire behaviour being observed the decision has been made to limit the number of responders exposed to this risk.

Ellsworth and Nadon signed the public notification, an uncharacteristic flourish for Parks Canada communications.

The first sentence of this 5:30 p.m. update—"first responders will start to be relocated"—inadvertently left an impression in some minds that Jasper was entirely empty of humans. Many people read no further and imagined a ghost town, silent and still as it prepared to meet its maker. If one had read the missive from top to bottom, however, that was clearly not the case.

Thirty minutes later, Ellsworth and Nadon returned with another update that outlined the situation in stark detail. Portions of the south fire had reached the outskirts of Jasper. Rain was expected that night. Firefighters remained in town combatting spot fires and maintaining sprinkler lines. In fact, they could do little else. They were finding that bucketing was ineffective against the inferno; heavy equipment being used to create a fireguard was pulled for safety; water bombers remained on the tarmac due to dangerous flying conditions.

At 7:10 p.m., Parks Canada provided yet another update, this one just three sentences long, with no sign-off:

> Around 6:40 pm this evening, wildfire reached the Jasper townsite. Parks Canada, the Municipality of Jasper, as well as responders from Alberta and other provinces are continuing with efforts to protect the town. Firefighters remain in town combatting multiple structural fires and are working to protect critical infrastructure.

Logan Ireland learned how the fire had progressed when he'd returned from a walk along the river in Valemount, where he and Kaylea had hunkered down to wait out the fire. She told him what she'd heard.

"You gotta call your parents," she said.

The first photo of Maligne Lodge in flames jumped around social media. Less than a week before, Logan had sat on its front porch with a coffee from Wicked Cup, its restaurant and coffee bar. "That was when you knew it was real," he says.

Indeed, the photo of Maligne Lodge confirmed peoples' worst fears. In Valemount, evacuees had gathered at a handful of local bars. They hugged. Most cried. They felt the pain of knowing the worst-case scenario had arrived. They didn't have any sense how bad the damage was, but hope evaporated.

Most assumed Jasper was in the process of being flattened—that not a structure would be left standing by morning. It was not difficult to imagine flames running from house to house, blowing through windows and doors like the grim reaper. Now where would they go? When, if ever, would they be allowed to return home?

Logan was exchanging texts with friends who'd scattered across Western Canada:

> Love you bro.
> Love you boys.
> Prayers up.
> Fuck my house.
> Hope your folks are doing alright.

"I went to sleep thinking the whole town was gone. I had this kind of emptiness," says Logan. "I remember thinking, 'I don't have a home.'"

All across Canada, people were assuming the Municipality of Jasper was about to be wiped off the map. Again, provincial leaders were on the outside looking in. Premier Danielle Smith continued her summer tour of community town halls across rural Alberta throughout the week. On Wednesday night, she had just wrapped up a question-and-answer session in the southern Alberta town of Taber when she found out the fire had breached Jasper. Unsure of the extent of the damage, she briefly continued toward Medicine Hat where she was scheduled to attend a parade and rodeo. As the severity of the fire became clearer, she stopped to record a brief video on her phone for social media before having her driver turn around so she could spend the night at her home in High River. She cleared her deck for the next day and planned to drive to Edmonton in the morning in the event she was called on to give a press conference.

Smith went to bed that night slightly optimistic that parts of Jasper would remain standing in the morning. She had learned how areas of Slave Lake were saved by structural firefighters' decisions to knock down burning homes and create built-in firebreaks in real time.

At 10 p.m., another update rolled in from Parks Canada, addressing the photos flying around the internet: yes, they were real. While the update reported significant losses, it was light on detail and gave readers no sense of how much of the town had been impacted. Firefighters were working to save as much as possible, it said.

"This will be the last update for tonight, July 24. We will provide further updates and information tomorrow."

* * *

The cedar-shake roofs were the easiest targets.

"That's when it started to turn into more of a rodeo," says Don Smith. "It was almost like if an ember looked at a cedar roof it would catch on fire."

The problem in neighbourhoods with even a mild density of cedar-shake roofs was the knock-on effect. Once one home caught fire, the radiant heat and 100 km/h wind sent debris and flames next door. One house in flames was enough to take down an entire block. Homes in those environments don't last as long as ordinary single-structure fires. Conditions were so hot, so cruel and inhospitable, that homes incinerated within minutes.

"It's almost like it's got its own agenda," says Smith. "Some of the big apartment buildings that burned down—I didn't even see them on fire. I just went back and they were gone."

Even if firefighters caught a cedar roof in the early stages of burning, they'd douse the flames, move to the next target, and by the time they returned the home would be on fire again. Once the flames broke through the roof and curled under the ceilings, the home didn't stand a chance.

Wednesday, July 24, 2024

In the midst of those multi-home fires, turning a hose on flames was like spitting into a campfire. Firefighters went into triage. If five houses were burning, they'd take out the last burning domino, using track hoes and feller bunchers (known to laymen as diggers), before it could spread and knock down the place next door.

The attitude, says Cornforth, was "we're not going to stop it . . . We'll knock that down and move on to the next thing."

Greg van Tighem, who had been at Jasper Park Lodge helping a group of firefighters from Parkland County and Grande Cache, evacuated around 6:30 Wednesday evening. Embers had started raining over the lodge; two buildings on the property had already caught fire. Van Tighem had been throwing plastic Muskoka chairs away from cabin porches before the fire arrived. "One got picked up and went about thirty feet in the air. That's when I started thinking that this might be getting a little too close," he says.

The scene was unlike anything any of the firefighters had seen before. Afterwards, some estimated winds reached more than 200 kilometres an hour—hurricane force.

Interestingly, some first responders don't remember the winds that night. Not everything registers in the heat of battle.

Others were more impressed by how loud the inferno was. "We had people say, 'They're running the trains,'" says Cornforth. "I said, 'No, that's the fire.' Trains had shut down. The roar was [the fire's] sound."

Firefighters who stayed that night by Jasper Park Lodge later told van Tighem that buildings would catch and be incinerated in seconds, fed by the wind. "They could hardly even stand up," he says. Fire leaped from tree to tree across the golf course, vaporizing a historic ten-bedroom cabin here, an eight-plex unit there. Dozens of staff rooms went down in the fire. A warehouse and the building holding golf maintenance equipment were incinerated.

The main lodge was saved partly by the good fortune of looking out on a lake, limiting how close the fire could get from one side.

Cornforth, whose team was responsible for guarding the structure, says the fire glanced on both sides of the property, but never managed to get too close to the building. The extensive sprinkler system wetting the structure no doubt played an important role.

Back in town, fire trucks and suppression vehicles whizzed through the streets, putting out infant roof fires before they could spread. Flames caught on the roof of Jasper's hospital. They were doused before it was able to expand.

There was nothing that could save the Cabin Creek neighbourhood, with all its cedar-shake shingles. It was wiped out.

St. Mary & St. George Anglican Church stood literally and, for many, figuratively, in the heart of Jasper on Miette Avenue. It was the first church in town, beginning as a log structure in 1914 and rebuilt from local materials in English Gothic revival fashion in 1928. In 1985, Alberta' ministry of culture had declared it a historic resource as an example of its style and one of the only remaining ecclesiastic buildings designed by Edmonton architect A. M. Calderon. A popular spot for mountain weddings, it was consumed by flames. Only its stone base remained standing.

The destruction of the church meant that the fire was right at the edge of the dozen-square-blocks that comprise Jasper's downtown core. Crews started noticing spot fires popping up on the roofs of businesses. Smith had been driving around town, yelling into a walkie-talkie, letting his colleagues know where new trouble spots were emerging starting. On several occasions, he missed turns because once familiar neighbourhoods had become unrecognizable.

As smoke plumed from a handful of businesses, Smith took control of the aerial truck, with its giraffe-like neck protruding several storeys high, to douse the fires from above downtown's two- and three-storey buildings. One business that had caught fire was immediately mowed down to prevent the flames from spreading; the roof of another building in the heart of the strip caught fire, but was suppressed before the flames could move further. Smith operated the truck for the better part of two hours.

Well after the sun had receded from the horizon, the firefighters took their first break since the action had ramped up. The wind had started blowing from the west, pushing the fire away from town and toward Maligne Valley.

Then, at some point after 10:30 p.m., the rain came.

Many firefighters tending to the downtown were initially unaware of the rain. The aerial truck, still operated by Smith, was continuing to bomb roofs across downtown.

"Anybody that was within 200 feet of me was soaked like right down to their underwear," says Smith. "We had no idea it was raining until we stopped, right? And then we're like, 'Holy shit, it's raining.'"

Conte and Cornforth had been standing together when the rain started, both also under the illusion they were catching spray from the aerial truck.

Along with the rain came fire crews from out of town, bringing Jasper's population from several dozen to over a hundred.

Even with the rain, the fight was far from over. Red-hot basements had turned into large hollowed-out ovens, laying side by side and emitting smoke. It nevertheless seemed as though the blaze had lost the initiative. Embers were no longer bombing the town; the howls were diminished.

"I knew we were out of that first wave of the firestorm," says Cornforth.

There was no rejoicing. Work continued. The new firefighters entering Jasper, unfamiliar with their surroundings, were shepherded to areas that needed attention.

That night, Cornforth, who was born and raised in Jasper, watched his childhood neighbourhood burn to the ground in forty-five minutes. St. Mary's & St. George's, where he had been baptized and where he had held his father's funeral, was gone.

Don Smith saw his sister-in-law's home burn over the course of two hours.

Eight members of the fire department lost their homes that night. Most watched them burn.

Conte saw his home go down that night. As he patrolled the streets of Jasper, he'd pass by every so often and find it closer to being gone. He'd didn't call for support to save it; the radiant heat was too strong in any event.

"It is what it is, right? We had so much on the go that night, and everything was changing so quickly. Didn't really have time to stop and ponder your own loss and what was going on," he says. "It was just, move on to the next."

Cornforth was with Conte when the chief's house caught fire. Few words were spoken. That was that.

"Those firefighters that lost their homes, they didn't get off the truck and walk away. They paused and then went at it again," says Cornforth.

By 3 a.m., although dozens of houses were still on fire, the wildfire had moved on. The population of firefighters had by then blown past 200. The rain continued through the dark of night. The rodeo was over.

"The part that was gonna burn had burned," says Smith.

CHAPTER 7

"BEYOND IMAGINATION"

The fire kicked our asses. It burned burned burned for two days then at 4 p.m. yesterday afternoon it came to town from Marmot Basin in 30 minutes. We stood no chance in the heat and wind until about 11 pm when the rain began and nine fire trucks from Alberta descended on us for support. The town has suffered catastrophic loss and we are not out of the woods yet but we did have some wins today. When we left, we still had a hospital, fire hall and water treatment plant which are mandatory for us to be able to stay and fight the fire.
—Text from unnamed wildfire fighter,
Thursday morning, July 25, 2024

When the sun rose over Jasper on Thursday morning, silence hung in the air like a haze.

Information about the fire emerged in fits and spurts. A video of a smouldering street, levelled to nothing, circulated on social media. Not even life-long residents could tell exactly where in town the video had been shot. Like all of the photos and videos that came to light that day, it failed to deliver any sense of the extent of the damage, beyond that it was bad.

"I'd already been through a bit of that remorse and grief for the whole town being gone," says Logan Ireland.

Officials were slow to fill the news vacuum. The Alberta government spent much of the morning waiting for Parks Canada and Jasper to decide which of them would be the first to speak to the public. Premier Danielle Smith arrived at her office, having driven from High River to Edmonton, and waited with her ministers for Parks Canada to offer up public communications before deciding their next move.

The premier had been a member of the Alberta legislature during the 2011 Slave Lake fire. She'd been a radio host during the Fort McMurray wildlife. In both instances, she'd observed what she felt was haphazard communication. In this instance, she had a statement prepared. "I knew that even though it was not our fire, and that in Jasper the reporting relationship was to Parks Canada . . . I knew that we couldn't allow for an information and communications gap," she says.

Parks Canada released its first statement Thursday morning at 10:30, reporting that much had been lost in Jasper, but much had been saved. The worst had passed; the rain had helped; 36,000 hectares (almost 90,000 acres) had been burned. But for all intents and purposes, it felt like communication for communication's sake. There was little to say. "While we understand people are desperate to know about the status of our community, homes, work places, businesses, and cherished places we will need some time to stabilize this incident as we access and assess structures," Parks Canada wrote.

The Alberta government announced twenty minutes later that the premier would speak at 11:30, an arrangement that was by no means coordinated between the two levels of government.

Standing behind the podium, Smith whipped through the beginning of her remarks with militaristic affect. About thirty seconds into the statement, as she expressed her sympathies to Jasper residents, her voice caught. "The feelings of loss and fear and loneliness must be overwhelming," she said, pausing to clear her throat. Her voice became less assertive. "But you are not alone. All Albertans are with you. The town of Jasper and the parks surrounding it have been a source of pride," she continued, pausing again to fully inhale.

A well-practised orator, Danielle Smith, considered even by her enemies to be among the more talented political communicators in the country, continued to choke through sentences as she described Jasper's mountains, valleys, and lakes. An aide placed a box of tissues on the podium. "And to those in Alberta and around the world who have . . ." she paused, her voice shaking, "experienced the magic of Jasper . . ." pausing again, "the magic is not lost and it never will be."

She was followed on the podium by sober-faced officials presenting a range of the potential damage, one so wide it was evident they didn't know how much of Jasper was gone: a third on the low end, but possibly half. Somewhere between 350 and 550 homes. A difference of 200 homes is hugely significant in a town with a total of 1,113 structures.

The Jasper wildfire triggered a reaction in the general public that previous wildfires had not. Most Canadians, even if they had never been to Jasper, had at least heard of it and seen pictures of it. No disrespect to Slave Lake, Fort McMurray, or Lytton, but most Canadians wouldn't be able to find those communities on a map, and fewer still would have dreamed of someday visiting them.

Especially online, the response to the fire and Smith's address was bewilderment, anger, and grief. There were calls for greater action on climate change. Confusion swirled over the jurisdictional intricacies of fighting the fire. Why wasn't the province in charge of a town that participates in provincial elections? Whose firefighting resources were responsible for putting out the fire? It was a black hole that got deeper the longer you looked. Jasper became a political football that day, and would remain one in the weeks following. Everyone wanted to lay blame for the devastation.

Park officials attempted to clamp down on photos and videos of ruins emerging through social media, partly due to fear that evacuated families would scroll to a photo of their childhood home reduced to a crater in the ground. The effort was futile, however well intentioned. Visuals of the town did land on social media, presumably from first responders scanning the destroyed neighbourhoods. Most images were of damage. Some showed that entire blocks of the town were razed.

"I grew up there and I didn't even recognize it," says Logan Ireland. "And then you'd see, 'Oh, there's the roundabout' and you'd have to backtrack and be like, 'Okay, they're right by what used to be the senior's lodge, and then that's Dr. Slack's house that is completely gone. . . . Oh, Scott Wilson's house is still there.'"

Brian Cornforth and many of his colleagues, finally aided by a firefighting force that had swollen to nearly 1,000 responders by Thursday, departed Jasper at 3 a.m. that morning. Don Smith and a number of Jasper volunteers left at 5 a.m. They were dehydrated, hungry, and depleted. They'd barely slept all week. Astonishingly, nobody left hurt.

The fire had subsided, but was still out of control. For the firefighters who remained, complacency wasn't an option given how the wind had behaved all week. The south and north fires had, by then, come within fifty meters of each other, but were holding far steadier than the days prior; on occasions it crept toward Pyramid Mountain, directly north of town. The cloud cover and weather conditions prevented Parks Canada from assessing the fire from above that day.

Regardless, as the text from the unnamed firefighter had noted, Jasper's critical infrastructure—its hospital, schools, firehall, and wastewater treatment plant—had survived the fire, along with the town's activity centre and main commercial strip. Losing the wastewater treatment plant would have effectively killed Jasper for at least three years. It would not have been able to support its own tiny population, let alone the 2.5 million visitors that come every year.

* * *

The Saturday after the fire, on an overcast morning, media and public officials were given their first tour of the town. For Richard Ireland, the previous five days had all blended into one. His townsfolk were scattered across Western Canada. He spent his time after the fire attempting to communicate the little information he had across print and televised media and through the town website. In his effort to be the steady hand at the wheel for his small community, he kept his eyes focused on the next televised interview or the next address to the community. He had little time for social media, knowing there was a chance he'd encounter a video he did not intend, nor want, to see. And even with a direct line to volunteer firefighters who knew where he lived and whom he'd known for years, Richard Ireland still didn't know whether his own home was still standing.

"I didn't personally want to know because I had other things that I had to focus on and I didn't want to get distracted by my own issue," he says, "for fear that my reaction would not be what it should be. It would, if not cripple me, it would perhaps at least diminish my capacity for the work that I had to do."

Before getting his first tour of Jasper that Saturday, Ireland stood alongside Premier Smith, federal ministers, and a small handful of other politicians as they fielded questions from reporters in Hinton near a set of trailers acting as an emergency-response headquarters. As the press conference wound down, Ireland remembers being asked what he expected to see when he re-entered Jasper.

"What I don't expect is any cameras," he said.

About an hour later, the convoy of vehicles arrived in Jasper, meandering through the untouched east side. Fences stood upright. Vacated homes exhibited no signs of damage. Riding in the lead vehicle, Ireland rounded a corner and took his first look at the smouldering pits where homes had stood days earlier. He could see his neighbour's home standing. Kevin's house had survived. Behind Kevin's house he could see his own back fence and his garage's roof. Had his home survived?

His house was not part of the predetermined tour route. But when the vehicle slowed to a stop, Ireland jumped out and ran toward his house. "I broke and said, 'I gotta go see.'"

When he arrived, all that remained was a column of cinder blocks protruding from the centre of the foundation. Ash and twisted, blackened metal sat inside the rectangular, concrete-walled hole where his home used to stand. The air outside was acrid from the toxic materials that had burned: microwaves, televisions, batteries.

Before anyone caught him, Ireland snapped a photo of Kevin's house with his phone and messaged it to his wife, asking her to send the news to their long-time neighbour. Don't share this with anyone else, he asked her.

He stood in front of his own home. He'd known it for almost seven decades. It was the place where a young Richard Ireland had scattered his toys; where he and his four siblings slept in bunk beds; where he raised his own two children and retreated after a long day in the mountains.

His moment alone was brief. Ireland was soon joined by Premier Smith, and federal and provincial emergency ministers. "This is your family home?" Smith asked him. Yes, for sixty-seven years, he answered. The premier responded with a yelp. An official shook his hand while Smith stood with a hand over her mouth. The moment of unscripted rawness did not seem to disturb Ireland. He had nothing to gain by calibrating his response. "I'm sorry, I didn't mean to make the tour about this," he said.

The group scanned the property for several minutes. Standing next to federal emergency preparedness minister Harjit Sajjan, Ireland spotted an old filing cabinet that days ago had held his income tax records. "You want 'em?" he said to Sajjan.

The town was thick with contradictions. A seemingly untouched car sitting in front of a pile of rubble; a pile of splintered wood where a restaurant once stood; its neighbour remained in pristine condition.

Even Ireland family's garage survived, protecting several bikes he would put to good use.

There were signs of firefighting activity in those areas. When Logan Ireland scanned his childhood home, he found the garden hose laying limp on the ground, evidence of what he believes was an effort to douse parts of the house before flames reached it. How else could a three-storey bonfire fail to swallow the Ireland's little garage? He and his father will likely never know.

"There's a lot of head scratchers, I'll tell you, in Jasper," says van Tighem, who, under normal circumstances, could accurately determine how some structures survived and others didn't based on FireSmart principles. "There's stuff that just does not make any sense. And like I said to a few people, don't even try and figure it out, because it just doesn't make sense the way buildings are there and others aren't."

"A house is totally burned to nothing—there's the foundation with rubble—and ten feet away is a plastic garden shed."

The Coveys had left their pet fish when they evacuated. That fish was the topic of several conversations with their daughter while they were away: "Is the fish going to be OK, Dad?" she asked. Over the week, one of Covey's friends on the emergency response team retrieved the fish. Until the family returned, the Covey fish became the wastewater treatment plant's emotional-support animal. Stories like that circulated for weeks.

The damage beyond the town boundary was also catastrophic. The horizon facing the town's main strip had been dramatically altered. With the morning sun rising from behind the jagged peaks, the silhouettes of thousands of burned-out trees stuck out of the ground like blackened matchsticks. Even from a distance, the forest floor was more visible without the foliage that had once shielded the ground from view.

While none of the first responders had been lost when the fire hit Jasper, tragedy struck just over a week later, a reminder of the dangers that remained out in the woods. On August 3, Parks Canada wildfire fighter Morgan Kitchen died when a tree fell on him as he worked at the wildfire complex. He was remembered by colleagues as a "brilliant personality with a nimble wit and encyclopedic knowledge of wide-ranging topics." His sense of humour "veered toward the outrageous and ridiculous," his obituary read, a beautiful and witty representation of the twenty-four-year-old's life.

Richard Ireland attended Kitchen's funeral in Calgary later that month. In case he was called upon to speak, he prepared a poem titled *Hero*. Ireland was a writer, not by trade, but by practice. He wrote all his speeches, updates and addresses over those months after the fire.

> Your son, your brother, your kin, your friend
> His gift to us shall have no end
> Last week, today, and each tomorrow
> His spirit lives: a Jasper hero

* * *

Where residents and tourists left a void in Jasper those first days and weeks, wildlife filled it.

Elk and grizzly bears wandered the streets less than forty-eight hours after the fire, unperturbed and perhaps delighted by the lack of human activity. The streets were theirs to roam, bushes theirs to munch.

Not all wildlife was unscathed, however. Assessing losses is a deeply unscientific process, says Erin Bayne, a biological sciences professor at the University of Alberta. Fires, especially of the magnitude in Jasper, entirely consume birds and small mammals and often leave no trace. Bears' remains are sometimes discovered, although rarely.

By Bayne's estimate, most of the birds in Jasper would have flown away. Terrestrial critters likely burrowed half a meter or so underground and waited out the flames. Birds that died would have been small juveniles, unable to fly; there were likely few at that time of year. Had the fire happened in June when many were still learning to fly, losses would have been "catastrophic."

Species such as the common nighthawk, a prairie bird, may become more common in the Jasper area now because of their preference for open spaces; certain species of woodpeckers also adore burned-out trees. On one occasion, Bayne walked through a recently burned forest and found a robin nesting.

Among Jasper's forest of woodland creatures, says Bayne, the elk would likely have fled to safety. They would likely have come back for the new foliage emerging from the soil after the fire. "The elk in Jasper are going to be ecstatic once it starts to grow back," he says, although they might be less pleased about having less foliage to shield them from predators.

Bears might be less pleased if the fire burned their dens, forcing them to possibly spend more time in the fall searching for a new place to hunker down for winter.

*   *   *

Jasper residents were allowed to return to town on August 16, nearly four weeks after their forced and, as it proved out, necessary evacuation. To the surprise of some, the day was a muted affair. There were no ribbon cuttings.

"It felt like a ghost town," says Logan Ireland, one of the few who returned that morning. People trickled in through the week. Others held off, not so much because of the emotional or psychological aspects of going home, although all that was in play; many simply didn't have a place to go. Unless residents were still in Hinton or Valemount, Jasper was at least four hours away by car—a trip that would double in time in the likely event a round-trip was required because of the lack of accommodation. Jasper's distance from urban life, viewed unanimously by residents as one of its greatest assets, had now become a problem.

Summer was already sliding into fall when the town cautiously rebooted its tourism industry. Half the busy season had by then washed away. Jasper's winter tourism season is muted compared to Banff, as fewer people are willing to wage battle with the Icefields Parkway. As a result, no business owners were particularly eager to reopen after the fire. The local economy isn't big enough to support small businesses without a steady flow of visitors.

Much of the town is now focused on rebuilding and the shape it will take. In mid-September, the federal government announced it will be ceding land-use planning to Jasper for the 30 percent of structures that had been destroyed, the first time in history the town had been granted such a responsibility.

Town council is intent on preserving its existing development guardrails. It will not permit ten-storey condos in Cabin Creek, nor will the town's compact boundary be expanding. But it will allow Jasper to reimagine its future and try to answer unresolved questions that have plagued it for decades, such as its chronically low vacancy rate and dearth of staff housing for seasonal workers. Parks' fingerprints would still be on the designs, although early guidelines loosened restrictions on secondary suites. Rebuilt homes are *required* to adhere to FireSmart principles: wood siding and roofing are outlawed ("This is a significant change and necessary to help protect Jasper in the long term," Parks Canada wrote); non-flammable buffer zones around homes have been mandated. Conifers have to be planted ten meters from buildings.

Rebounding will be an immense task: insurers calculated $880 million in losses, among the costliest disasters in Canadian history.

One feature of the town that was not changed by the fire is its vulnerability to another one. Due to the shift in wind that sent the fire north toward Hinton, the wildfire never ventured into the thicket of mature lodgepole pines west of Jasper from where locals had long expected it to arrive. The south is the only threat that has been eliminated, although wind from that direction was relatively unlikely.

"That west valley is still our biggest threat," Conte said. While there are exceptions to the rule, the wind frequently travels from that valley into Jasper.

It raises a challenging question for Parks Canada, which maintains its prescribed burning and thinning efforts had been sufficient leading up to the fire. Many believe the perimeter around the townsite should have been thinned out even more, and should be in the future given the threat of another fire.

"In my mind, I always wanted to go further," said Greg van Tighem, the former fire chief, although tree-thinning in the national park went beyond his jurisdiction. He noted there are limited options for towns looking to ward off fires from breaching their boundaries. "The only way to do that is to seriously reduce the fuel load around communities and also build non-combustible neighbourhoods. Sounds easy, sounds simple, but it's definitely not easy."

To that extent, fire specialists descended upon Jasper in the disaster's aftermath to understand what exactly occurred over those three days. Their findings will undoubtedly be integrated into heavily researched post-mortems perhaps a year or more down the line.

In the interim, anecdotes were helpful in drawing general conclusions. The sheer power of the inferno alarmed several of the firefighters who were inside it. Even the staunchest FireSmart devotees, such as van Tighem, aren't certain a gold-standard town would have survived without significant loss. "What came through there was just so intense. It was ridiculous. It was beyond imagination," he says.

Rumours swirled of mini tornados occurring in the storm. The winds seemed unnatural to Jasper. Mike Flannigan of Thompson Rivers University and other researchers quickly identified the conditions as those found in pyrocumulonimbus clouds, a phenomenon in which thunder storms are created by the intense heat from wildfires. Informally called pyroCbs, they're driven by intense heat, causing air to rise above the fire; when it reaches colder temperatures higher in the atmosphere, the circulation of air makes the atmosphere unstable, creating thunderstorm-like conditions. These fires generate their own lightning and tornados. Some call them fire clouds. They often exhibit erratic winds that generate dense smoke; they're almost impossible to combat from above.

PyroCbs are perhaps why, when Jasper went from day to night in the early evening of July 24, firefighters felt like they were in a different weather system. It's probably because they were.

In Canada's growing era of wildfire and climate change, these phenomena have become an increasingly common symptom of large blazes: in 2023, 140 pyroCbs were recorded in Canada, nearly triple the previous record, according to a paper authored by Flannigan and seventeen other researchers. Nowhere in the world do these conditions occur more frequently.

Considering the sum total of events that led to the devastation in Jasper, Flannigan was unequivocal in his assessment of why winds were so strong and why the fire moved so much faster than expected. "If I was to say, 'What was the cause of this?' I'd say 89 percent pyroCb, 1 or 2 percent Mountain Pine Beetle, 5 to 8 percent fire suppression," he says. "It was the extreme fire weather."

For all the talk of rebirth, the thirty-five-kilometre stretch and the thousands of acres from Jasper southward down the Icefield Parkway to Mount Kerkeslin will not be the place it once was, at least not for a long time. Landon Shepherd, who flew over the damage more than thirty times after the fire, describes the aftermath as a "path of destruction." Healthy, hundreds-of-years-old Douglas-firs ripped from the base of their roots. Swaths of land where 100 percent of trees were killed, even near wetlands. The experts studying the aftermath, says Shepherd, expressed to him they had never witnessed this level of severity.

"Sometimes my adjectives fail me," he says.

In theory, the forest should undergo a decades-long rebirth. The pinecone seeds that bombed toward the ground through thousand-degree heat *should* grow into a healthy, dense forest of trees, fed by the nutrient-rich soil. Every tree that falls to the ground should add to the ingredients needed for regrowth. With multiple years of rain in the park, the regrowth will take off. When it's fully grown, more than two decades after the fire, the forest will indeed look as it should: well-spaced and healthy. Even less than a month after the fire, razed stretches along the parkway were covered in a soft layer of grass the colour of a golf green, a stark contrast to the thousands of splitting black tree carcasses standing in neat rows.

But there are no guarantees the regeneration will unfold in typical fashion. The knock-on effects of a warmer, drier climate allow for alternative scenarios. Researchers are closely watching to see if Jasper's forests rebound or if the landscapes burn again too soon, a scenario that could see it become a savannah in which the forest can only be replaced by being replanted. There are no guarantees that the long intervals between wildfires Gerald Tande noted in his 1977 study will resume. They could become terrifyingly short. "It can get to the point where no trees start to grow," says the University of Alberta's Bayne.

Much was made in the months following the Jasper fire about the Mountain Pine Beetle and the thousands of dead pine trees across the valley that were its legacy. The species ravaged forests across Western Canada from 1999 to 2015. (Interestingly, the beetle, too, is a product of climate change as warmer winters in the 1990s provided a more hospitable environment for the pests. Frigid winters had thwarted their advance until then.)

Flannigan believes the pine beetle "is a bit of a red herring in this case." Pines killed by the beetle will turn orange and red as the tree dies and the needles are tinder-dry, but still alive, leaving them in their most flammable and dangerous state. But once the coloured tints recede, the dying needles fall off and the lodgepole is killed, the trees begin to fall to the ground where they rot. This is called the grey stage. These trees are flammable, yes, but because so many lay on the forest floor and burn with pace, they support active surface fires, not the atmosphere-licking crown fire that sped toward Jasper on July 24.

"This is much less flammable. (It's) really hard to get a crown fire, almost impossible, because the needles really are the fuel," says Flannigan.

* * *

The political and jurisdictional conversations that popped up on social media in the immediate wake of the wildfire have since migrated to Ottawa. Jasper has become such a hot-button issue that members of Parliament summoned Environment Minister Steven Guilbeault, Parks Canada Incident Commander Landon Shepherd, and Andrew Campbell, senior vice president of operations for Parks Canada, to a committee meeting on the factors that led to the wildfire.

Between six-minute questioning blocks and hyper-partisan attacks, it was immediately apparent the forum was not built for such a discussion. In one instance, as Shepherd offered a detailed look at Parks Canada's response to the several fires that flickered to life on July 22, the commander was cut off so the committee could move to the next MP's questions. Shepherd and Campbell, neither of them a politician, spoke slowly and disputed claims raised by Conservative MPs intent on placing blame on the sitting Liberal government. Perhaps the only newsworthy statement to emerge from the meeting was that Parks Canada may consider creating larger buffer zones around municipalities. Summers are becoming more challenging, said Shepherd. "Our jobs have been getting harder."

Richard Ireland, for his part, wanted nothing to do with it. "The present atmosphere of finger-pointing, blaming and both partial and misinformation is, from my perspective, beyond mercy an annoying distraction," he said at a media event, reported by the *Jasper Fitzhugh*. "It delays healing. It introduces fresh wounds and fosters division, precisely at a time when we need recovery and unity."

As fall arrived in Alberta, serious questions about the wildfire remained unanswered. What exactly were the conditions inside the inferno? Was there anything that could've remotely been done?

Despite the dearth of answers, one thing is certain: Jasper won't be the last community devastated by wildfire. "I can't tell you when. I can't tell you where, but this will happen again," says Flannigan.

* * *

The media continued to report on Jasper's rebuilding decisions and political controversies through the fall. The issues being discussed at town council and with Parks Canada are undoubtedly important to the town's future, but many people were still trying to get their lives back together and frankly didn't have time to concern themselves with larger questions. Three-hour administrative meetings are difficult to schedule amid afternoons on the phone with insurance companies or wrestling matches with a troubled balance sheet. People in Jasper were trying to live their lives, rebuild their homes.

Greg van Tighem's property, sitting directly across the street from Richard Ireland's now-empty lot, survived the fire. Brian Cornforth's eighty-eight-year-old mother moved in with him, having lost her residence.

Logan Ireland's apartment escaped unscathed, allowing him and Kaylea to move back early on. He landed a job in town helping with the recovery efforts.

Mathew Conte, left without his home, spent the first month after the fire in Hinton as he helped manage the unified command.

Bob Covey and his family were reunited with their fish in August.

Many of the unhoused bunked with friends and family on returning to town. Others decided to take the insurance money and set up life elsewhere.

There was a strangeness and a deep sadness to life in Jasper in the months after the fire. Stavro Korogonas, the owner of a local pizzeria who lost his home, says "people have talked about losing limbs and they've talked about how they can still feel their toes or feel an itch sometimes. It was like that. It's gone, but you can still feel it there."

Korogonas plans to manage his business from Kelowna over the winter. He hardly slept the first months after the fire, frequently waking up in the middle of the night remembering items his family had lost. Days blended into each other as he made a flurry of decisions on how to reboot the business and get on with his life. Grief often visited him without asking. By late September, his wife still hadn't visited town. For her, he says, it would be too much, too soon. "It's all-consuming for the most part. It's really hard to let go of, I'll tell you that much. Really hard to get used to it not being there."

The firefighters in Jasper cope in their own ways. Some struggle with decisions they made that night. Others are haunted by the whole experience. "We have a lot of younger, newer members," Don Smith says. "They thought they had an idea of how this would go, but I'm pretty sure reality was much more shocking to them."

Smith, a veteran firefighter is largely unperturbed by what the fire put him through, but every once in a while something will catch him by surprise, like a sudden rustling in the woods or a conversation with a Jasperite. "A parent of one of your younger firefighters, they say something like, 'Thank you for keeping my son safe,'" he says. "It hits you like a ton of bricks in the forehead."

The Thursday morning after the fire, Meg Markulin woke up with cramps. They were minor enough to avoid a fuss, significant enough to merit notice. By 9 a.m., she and Terry decided to visit the hospital.

The doctors told her she wasn't going into labour; she could be back in a day, several days, or the next week. The baby would come when it wanted.

Meg and Terry drove back to her sister's place, taking the long way home. By the time they were close to pulling around to the house, her contractions started. Terry whipped the car around and drove back to the hospital. Just after arriving, Meg's water broke.

Terry took control of both their phones, texting family and friends that the baby was on the way. Outside the room, he got a call. It was the owner of Wicked Cup, the cafe in Maligne Lodge that was now nothing more than scorched concrete and twisted steel. Terry recalls the conversation:

> Terry, how you doing?
> Oh, just my wife's giving birth right now.
> Oh, cool.
> I saw your restaurant burned down.
> Yeah, kind of shit. Well, we'll have to check in with each other later.

Meg's birth progressed quickly. That morning, in Kelowna General Hospital, where a wildfire had burned a year earlier across the lake, Atticus Wren Chauncey, all six pounds and two ounces of him, was born. There were few things that could wash away the events from the night before. This one could, and did.

"Everything I thought I had after that Wednesday, thinking that our house was gone, Meg was my everything," says Terry.

When Jasper reopened to residents three weeks later, there were only three cars ahead of Terry waiting at the park gates. He didn't know why the impulse to witness the damage was so strong, other than desperately wanting to understand the state of his property.

When he arrived through the undamaged north side of Jasper, the town still smelled like burned plastic. His house was standing, but he feared the backside sustained more damage than he'd initially known. Sitting alone in his car, he cried.

He didn't let it last. He stepped out and walked to the front door. Early the following week, Terry, Meg and Atticus returned to Jasper. They bunked with a friend while cleaners scrubbed their house from top to bottom. Their nursery needed to be replaced—the new crib and toys all sustained smoke damage beyond repair.

That their home was largely spared did not keep them from mourning. For years, Terry and Meg had gone on evening walks on a loop, spanning about eight blocks through old Jasper homes. Only about three of those blocks remained. Friends who'd lost everything had decided not to come back. Meg had to shift her expectations of what her first months of motherhood would be like. "I kind of expected to show off the baby when we did have it," she says. "We're losing out on a part of the community that we were really looking forward to in our future. That was devastating for me."

A long list of tasks lays ahead of Terry and Meg, not least rebooting their careers. Some of the tasks are daunting, others welcome. One day while he was looking at his property, Terry noticed the grass had grown long. Whether out of masculine instinct or a craving for normalcy, he pulled out the lawnmower and got to work.

"It was one of the happiest feelings," he says, "of just having that time to not think about anything and just say, 'Let's mow some grass.'"

ABOUT THE AUTHOR

Matthew Scace is a journalist for the *Calgary Herald* and *Calgary Sun*, and has written for several publications including *The Globe and Mail*, *National Post* and *Vancouver Sun*. *Fire on the Mountain* is his first book. He lives in Calgary.

GIVE A THOUGHTFUL GIFT

1 YEAR PRINT & DIGITAL SUBSCRIPTION

**SAVE 20% OFF THE $19.95
PER ISSUE COVER PRICE**

- **Four** print books
- **Free** home delivery
- Plus **four** eBooks
- **Free** digital access to all SQ publications
- Automatic renewal

DELIVERY & PAYMENT DETAILS

Subscriber Info

NAME:
ADDRESS:
EMAIL: PHONE:

Payment Options

- Enclose a cheque or money order for $67.99 (includes HST) made out to Sutherland House Inc. Send to Sutherland House, 304-416 Moore Ave, Toronto, ON, Canada M4G 1C9
- Debit my Visa or MasterCard for $67.99 (includes HST)

CARD NUMBER: ____ ____ ____ ____   **CVV:** ___
EXPIRY DATE: __ / __   **AMOUNT: $**
PURCHASER'S NAME: **SIGNATURE:**

OR SUBSCRIBE ONLINE AT SUTHERLANDQUARTERLY.COM

GET THE WHOLE STORY

1 YEAR PRINT & DIGITAL SUBSCRIPTION

SAVE 20% OFF THE $19.95 PER ISSUE COVER PRICE

- **Four** print books
- **Free** home delivery
- Plus **four** eBooks
- **Free** digital access to all SQ publications
- Automatic renewal

DELIVERY & PAYMENT DETAILS

Subscriber Info

NAME:
ADDRESS:
EMAIL: PHONE:

Payment Options

- Enclose a cheque or money order for $67.99 (includes HST) made out to Sutherland House Inc. Send to Sutherland House, 304-416 Moore Ave, Toronto, ON, Canada M4G 1C9
- Debit my Visa or MasterCard for $67.99 (includes HST)

CARD NUMBER: ____ ____ ____ ____   **CVV:** ___
EXPIRY DATE: __ / __   **AMOUNT:** $
PURCHASER'S NAME: **SIGNATURE:**

OR SUBSCRIBE ONLINE AT SUTHERLANDQUARTERLY.COM